200
NIGHTTIME
PRAYERS
for
Girls

HILARY BERNSTEIN

200 NIGHTTIME PRAYERS for Girls

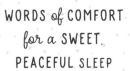

WORDS of COMFORT
for a SWEET,
PEACEFUL SLEEP

BARBOUR **kidz**
A Division of Barbour Publishing

Cover Design: Greg Jackson, Thinkpen Design

Published by Barbour Publishing, Inc., 1810 Barbour Drive, Uhrichsville, Ohio 44683, www.barbourbooks.com

Our mission is to inspire the world with the life-changing message of the Bible.

Member of the
Evangelical Christian
Publishers Association

Printed in China.

000549 0121 HA

When you lie down,
YOU WILL NOT BE AFRAID;
when you lie down,
YOUR SLEEP WILL BE SWEET.

PROVERBS 3:24 NIV

Do you ever have trouble falling asleep? You're not alone. Life is filled with all sorts of things that can leave you tossing and turning at night.

When you can't fall asleep—or stay asleep—it might feel like you're all alone with your problems and cares. But you're not! Your heavenly Father is right there, knowing exactly what you're thinking. And He's listening to your prayers and loving you so very much.

You don't have to wonder what He thinks about you or what He'd love to tell you—because He *has* told you in the Bible. As you dig into His Word with these two hundred bedtime prayers, you'll be able to let His truth soak into your soul. It's amazing how His Word can calm your fears, reassure you of His love, and fill your nights with sweet sleep. Snuggle up with this book and get ready for a night of peaceful rest.

Sweet dreams!
HILARY BERNSTEIN

JESUS LOVES ME

I pray that Christ may live in your hearts by faith. I pray that you will be filled with love. I pray that you will be able to understand how wide and how long and how high and how deep His love is. I pray that you will know the love of Christ. His love goes beyond anything we can understand.
EPHESIANS 3:17–19 NLV

Father God, Your love is amazing. And Jesus' love for me is way beyond what I can even start to wrap my brain around. Jesus loves me. *Me!* I don't need to do anything on my own to earn His love. All I need is to believe in Him and accept His love as a beautiful gift. Thank You! Please help me realize how very much He loves me. In Jesus' name I pray, amen.

SAFE AND PROTECTED

I love You, O Lord, my strength. The Lord is
my rock, and my safe place, and the One Who
takes me out of trouble. My God is my rock,
in Whom I am safe. He is my safe-covering,
my saving strength, and my strong tower.
I call to the Lord, Who has the right
to be praised. And I am saved
from those who hate me.
PSALM 18:1–3 NLV

O Lord, I love You! It's a big relief to have You as my strength, my rock, my safe place. When I'm in trouble, You help me. Sometimes it's obvious that I have enemies, and when I do, I'll trust You to protect me. As I fall asleep tonight, please help me sleep peacefully, knowing You care about me every minute of every day. In Jesus' name I pray, amen.

NO WORRIES

So put away all pride from yourselves.
You are standing under the powerful hand
of God. At the right time He will lift you
up. Give all your worries to Him
because He cares for you.
1 PETER 5:6–7 NLV

Father, knowing that You care for me changes my life. I'm so thankful I can tell You anything and everything that's on my mind. I know You'll listen to me and help. Many things are worrying me right now. Could You please help me? I know I can't handle all that I'm facing and feeling on my own, but I know You can. You're powerful enough to do so much more than I can even imagine. I trust You'll work out all the details. Please help me trust You completely. In Jesus' name I pray, amen.

MORE THAN SKIN DEEP

*But the LORD said to him, "Pay no
attention to how tall and handsome he is.
I have rejected him, because I do not judge
as people judge. They look at the outward
appearance, but I look at the heart."*
1 SAMUEL 16:7 GNT

Father God, I admit it's hard not to focus on what
people look like. Sometimes I judge myself, and
I don't like what I see in the mirror even though
You created me and You see what's inside of me.
It's also really hard not to judge other people
by what they look like. I know I shouldn't, but
I do. Please help me to see what's inside others
so I can make wise choices about my friends.
Please help me to look deeper than what's on
the outside. In Jesus' name I pray, amen.

A GOOD WORK

God began doing a good work in you,
and I am sure he will continue it until it is
finished when Jesus Christ comes again.
PHILIPPIANS 1:6 NCV

Father, sometimes when I look at my life, it doesn't seem like it is full of good things. Some days are just crummy. But I get excited to know that You've started doing a good work in me. And You'll even finish that good work in me! I don't have to worry about perfecting what You've started, because You're the One who can do it all. Please help me not to get in Your way! Please open my eyes so I can see the good things You're already doing in me. In Jesus' name I pray, amen.

SPEAK UP!

"Speak up for people who cannot speak for themselves. Protect the rights of all who are helpless. Speak for them and be a righteous judge. Protect the rights of the poor and needy."
PROVERBS 31:8-9 GNT

Father God, thank You for giving me a voice! You've given me thoughts and words I can use to say what I think and to speak up for others too. Please open my eyes so I can see who needs help. I pray that I'll be a kind friend to other girls who are left out. Please help me to include outsiders and to treat everyone with kindness, no matter what they look like or sound like, or what they can or cannot do. Even though I'm just little old me, I trust You'll use me in a big way in someone else's life. In Jesus' name I pray, amen.

TOMORROW

You don't even know what your life tomorrow will be! You are like a puff of smoke, which appears for a moment and then disappears.
JAMES 4:14 GNT

Lord, it's hard for me to remember that the problems I have today won't last forever. There's no way I could ever know what tomorrow will be like! I kind of wish I did. But I'm going to choose to trust You. And as much as I wonder what will happen tomorrow—or next week or next month or next year—I don't have to worry. I know You're in control, and You have a wonderful plan. Help me to see You at work instead of getting discouraged or frustrated when things don't go my way—and please help me to trust You more and more. Amen.

AFRAID? OR STRONG AND BRAVE?

"Remember that I commanded you to be strong and brave. Don't be afraid, because the LORD your God will be with you everywhere you go."
JOSHUA 1:9 NCV

Father, I'm so thankful I can trust You. And I'm so thankful You're in control. Because, Lord, I'm scared! I don't want to do what I have to do. I don't feel like being brave. In fact, I'm so nervous, I feel like I just want to hide. But I know I need to be brave. I need courage to face what I don't want to face. And I need to remember what's true: You're with me wherever I go. I don't have to be afraid or discouraged. Through You, I can be strong and brave. Please help me find my courage and strength in You! Amen.

MY MOUTH AND MY HEART

If you say with your mouth that Jesus is Lord, and believe in your heart that God raised Him from the dead, you will be saved from the punishment of sin. When we believe in our hearts, we are made right with God. We tell with our mouth how we were saved from the punishment of sin.
ROMANS 10:9–10 NLV

Jesus, I do say that You are Lord! And I truly believe in my heart of hearts that God raised You from the dead and that You're living right now. Thank You that You save me when I say that You're my Lord. And thank You that when I believe in You, You make me right with You. Thank You for saving me from the punishment of sin. What You've done for me is absolutely amazing! In Jesus' name I pray, amen.

I TRUST YOU!

*Some trust in their war chariots and
others in their horses, but we trust in
the power of the LORD our God.*
PSALM 20:7 GNT

Father, when I look around me every day, I see
people trusting in all sorts of things—friends,
clothes, belongings, grades, vacations, and themselves. But why trust in any of that? What can a
thing or even a person really do? I don't want to
trust in the things of this world. I don't want to
love something or someone that will come and
go. And I definitely don't want to trust in myself.
I do trust You though. I know You're the Lord
of all and are completely powerful. Thank You
that You're worthy of my trust! In Jesus' name
I pray, amen.

BEING A FOLLOWER

*So we must be more careful to
follow what we were taught.
Then we will not stray
away from the truth.*
HEBREWS 2:1 NCV

Father God, I'm so glad I've been taught Your truth. Not only have I heard it, but I believe it! I want to be obedient to You and Your Word. I want to follow You. And I don't want to stray. Even when I'm pushed and pulled to be more like the world, I want to be more like You. I don't want to fall into the trap of doing things to fit in with my friends. And I don't want to do what's popular if it doesn't follow Your truth. Please help me bravely live for You. Keep me close to You and help me remember how Your Word teaches me to live. In Jesus' name I pray, amen.

HERE I AM!

Then I heard the voice of the Lord, saying,
"Whom should I send? Who will go for Us?"
Then I said, "Here am I. Send me!"

ISAIAH 6:8 NLV

Father, You are awesome. You've always existed. You've always had a plan for everything and everyone. Even me. Sometimes I wonder if You can use me to do big things for You. But as long as I listen to You, obey Your commands, and do Your work, You can and will use me. That's amazing! I pray that You'll give me strength to do what You ask. When I feel scared, please give me courage. When I doubt what I should do, please make my way clear. When I'm tempted to stick to what's comfortable, please help me choose to obey You. Here I am. Send me! In Jesus' name I pray, amen.

PLEASE FORGIVE ME

I do not understand what I do;
for I don't do what I would like to do,
but instead I do what I hate.
ROMANS 7:15 GNT

Father, I sinned against You today—and I really, really regret it. Please forgive me! I wish I didn't sin so much. I wish I would obey You more. I wish I could always make good decisions. I get so mad at myself when I know what I should do and choose to do something else. I pray that tomorrow I'll please You in all I think, say, and do. I want to start living for You, not for myself. In Jesus' name I pray, amen.

STOP TRYING

Be quiet and know that I am God.
PSALM 46:10 NLV

Father, I want to be a good girl even when it's hard. The amazing thing, though, is that You'll love me no matter what. I don't have to do anything to make You love me. In fact, in Your Word, You tell me to be quiet and know that You are God. That means I don't have to do or say anything. It's so hard not to strive to make You love me. But I don't have to do anything to earn Your favor! Instead of doing or saying good things and trying to make You love me, tonight I want to be close to You. In this quiet place, please help me to know You are God. In Jesus' name I pray, amen.

TRUST AND LOVE

This is what He said we must do: Put your
trust in the name of His Son, Jesus Christ,
and love each other. Christ told us to do this.
The person who obeys Christ lives by the
help of God and God lives in him.
We know He lives in us by the
Holy Spirit He has given us.
1 JOHN 3:23–24 NLV

Lord Jesus, I put my trust in You! I want to obey
what You've commanded. I pray that Your Spirit
will clearly guide me and help me live out Your
commands every day. You lived a life of love. I
want to do the same, even when it's not easy.
Please help Your love guide my life and be
noticeable in what I say and do. Thank You for
living in me! In Your precious name I pray, amen.

ALL YOUR HEART

Trust in the LORD with all your heart.
Never rely on what you think you know.
Remember the LORD in everything you do,
and he will show you the right way.
PROVERBS 3:5-6 GNT

Father, I hate to admit it, but sometimes I rely on what I think I know. I think I know the right way to do something or what I should say or think. I try to figure things out on my own and live my own way. But when I do that, I'm really just trusting in myself—not You. But Lord, I need You! I want to trust You with all my heart! I want to remember You in everything I do. It's amazing that when I remember and trust You, You show me the right way. Thank You that You're worthy of my trust! In Jesus' name I pray, amen.

WHAT SHOULD I WEAR?

*"And why worry about clothes? Look how
the wild flowers grow: they do not work or
make clothes for themselves. . . . It is God
who clothes the wild grass—grass that is
here today and gone tomorrow,
burned up in the oven. Won't he be
all the more sure to clothe you?"*
MATTHEW 6:28, 30 GNT

Lord, You promised that I don't have to worry
about what I wear. That's so different from the
focus of the world! But just like You dress flowers
so beautifully, You'll dress me too. I pray that
I'll be content with what I wear and that I'll
modestly protect my body. Please help me see
and be thankful for the wonderful ways You
actually do bring outfits and clothing into my
life—ways that I don't have to worry about or
consider. You are so good to me! Amen.

BULLIED

But the saving of those who are right with God is from the Lord. He is their strength in time of trouble. The Lord helps them and takes them out of trouble. He takes them away from the sinful, and saves them, because they go to Him for a safe place.

PSALM 37:39–40 NLV

Father God, the bullies in my life plan and do and say such horrible things. My heart feels broken, and I just want to cry. Please remind me that You don't see me the same way they do. And most people don't see me that way either. You're my strength when it feels like I don't have any. Can You please keep me safe from these bullies? I want to grow closer to You in this awful time—You are my safe place. When I'm in trouble, please help me! In Jesus' name I pray, amen.

CHOSEN BY YOU

God had already decided that through Jesus Christ he would make us his children—this was his pleasure and purpose. Let us praise God for his glorious grace, for the free gift he gave us in his dear Son!
EPHESIANS 1:5-6 GNT

Father, I don't understand Your plans or Your choices. But even when I can't understand something, I can still be thankful. Thank You for choosing to make me Your child through Jesus Christ! You could choose absolutely anyone (and You do!), so to know that You've chosen *me* is absolutely amazing. Thank You that choosing me was Your pleasure and purpose. You are so kind. I praise You for Your glorious grace, and I thank You for the free gift of it through Jesus. I don't deserve it, and I could never earn it, but I'm thankful for it! In Jesus' name I pray, amen.

THE PURSUIT OF PEACE

Would you like to enjoy life? Do you want long life and happiness? Then keep from speaking evil and from telling lies. Turn away from evil and do good; strive for peace with all your heart.
PSALM 34:12–14 GNT

Heavenly Father, I really do want to enjoy life! And I do want a long life and happiness! But sometimes it's so tough to live at peace with other people. I want to do good though. I want to strive for peace with all my heart. In the heat of the moment, it's hard to remember that what I say matters. But the words I choose have so much power. Please use me to be kind and to calm people. Please keep me from lying or saying bad things about others. Please use me as a peacemaker! In Jesus' name I pray, amen.

WATCH YOURSELF!

Brothers and sisters, if someone in your group does something wrong, you who are spiritual should go to that person and gently help make him right again. But be careful, because you might be tempted to sin, too.
GALATIANS 6:1 NCV

Father, I found out that one of my friends did something wrong. The thing is, I don't know if they're even sorry. They almost seem to enjoy what they've done. I'm upset by their sin—and I don't want to follow them. Could You please help me? I want to follow Your Word and try to help them make things right. But I'm worried I'll be tempted by what they're doing. Could You please keep me from doing wrong? I love You and want to please You with my decisions, Lord. I want to do what's right in Your eyes. In Jesus' name I pray, amen.

GOTTA HAVE FAITH

Faith means being sure of the things we hope for and knowing that something is real even if we do not see it.
HEBREWS 11:1 NCV

Father God, I come to You tonight, but I have to admit that sometimes I don't always know You're real. When You seem quiet, it's hard to remember that You're the living God. I want to believe in You. Please help me keep my faith in You. Even when I don't feel like You're there, please help me remember that faith is not a feeling. You're real, and that doesn't depend on whether I can see or feel or hear You. You're here. I can see proof that You're real in the world around me today. Thank You for loving me even when I'm tempted to doubt You. In Jesus' name I pray, amen.

DIFFERENT THAN THE WORLD

*But Noah pleased the LORD. . . . Noah did
everything the LORD commanded him.*
GENESIS 6:8; 7:5 NCV

Lord God, You have a wonderful way of knowing
who loves and obeys You. Even though Noah
lived in a wicked world, He still honored and
obeyed You. In fact, He did everything You
commanded Him, no matter what others around
him might have said or done. And You knew
it. When Noah followed and pleased You, he
found favor in Your eyes. Just like Noah, I feel
like I'm living in a wicked world. I pray that even
if I'm completely different from everyone else
around me because I obey You, I'll obey You
anyway. I want to follow You and do all that You
command me to do. I want to trust You. I love
You! In Jesus' name I pray, amen.

A LIVING HOPE

Let us give thanks to the God and Father of our Lord Jesus Christ! Because of his great mercy he gave us new life by raising Jesus Christ from death. This fills us with a living hope, and so we look forward to possessing the rich blessings that God keeps for his people. He keeps them for you in heaven, where they cannot decay or spoil or fade away.

1 PETER 1:3-4 GNT

Father, thank You for Your mercy. And thank You for new life and a hope that is real and living. As I hope in You, I wait and look forward to what I know will definitely come. Those treasures in heaven won't ever fade or spoil! Even though it may seem like a long time until I go to heaven, I can start looking forward to it now. In Jesus' name I pray, amen.

WHAT DO YOU THINK?

*Be careful how you think;
your life is shaped by your thoughts.*
PROVERBS 4:23 GNT

Father God, sometimes I forget how important my thoughts are. What I think, I end up believing. And what I believe shapes my life. My thoughts seem to go all over the place—every day and even moment by moment they seem to change! Some days it feels like I'm on a wild roller-coaster ride. Instead of trusting my ever-changing thoughts, I pray that I'll be careful about what I think about. Please help me keep bad influences out and cling to the good influences that please You. Please give me wisdom to know what thoughts need to stay and which ones need to go. In Jesus' name I pray, amen.

BECOMING A DO-GOODER

We must not become tired of doing good.
We will receive our harvest of eternal life
at the right time if we do not give up.
GALATIANS 6:9 NCV

Father God, sometimes it feels like I try so hard to do good—to do my best, to be a good example of what it's like to follow You, and to make life better for other people. But all of that goodness wears me out. I get tired! Please help me keep doing good. I really don't want to give up and stop doing good things. I love You and I want to serve You with my life! In Jesus' name I pray, amen.

GET WELL SOON

LORD, have mercy on me because I am weak.
Heal me, LORD, because my bones ache.
PSALM 6:2 NCV

Father, I haven't been feeling very good lately. I know all things happen for a reason, but Father, I wish I didn't have to feel so yucky! I pray that You'll heal me. Please help me feel better. When I'm tempted to worry about what's wrong, please fill me with peace. When I want to complain about how bad I feel, please help me keep a good attitude. And I pray that I can get plenty of rest and feel like myself again. In Jesus' name I pray, amen.

NOT MY OWN

Don't you know that your body is the temple of the Holy Spirit, who lives in you and who was given to you by God? You do not belong to yourselves but to God; he bought you for a price. So use your bodies for God's glory.
1 CORINTHIANS 6:19-20 GNT

Lord, sometimes it's hard to honor You with my body. Impurity is everywhere I look. Yet as uncommon as purity seems today, Your truth hasn't changed. My body is a temple of the Holy Spirit. Your Spirit is living inside of me—You've given Him as proof that I'm Yours. As much as I'm tempted to do whatever I'd like, I need to honor You in everything. My body's not my own! Help me remember that I was bought at a huge price—Christ's very life. In His name I pray, amen.

TRUST

Trust in the LORD and do good; live in the land and be safe. Seek your happiness in the LORD, and he will give you your heart's desire.
PSALM 37:3-4 GNT

Father, the thought of seeking my happiness in You is special! I can completely enjoy You—enjoy being with You and enjoy getting to know You more. As I find my happiness in You more and more, I naturally trust You more and more. And trusting in You adds peace to my life. Thank You that I don't have to worry about what could happen. As I trust in You and delight myself in You, so many great things happen—I end up doing good, I'm faithful to You, I'm safe, and a huge bonus is that You'll give me the desires of my heart. Thank You that I can trust You, Father! Amen.

WALKING THE WALK

*As you have put your trust in Christ Jesus
the Lord to save you from the punishment
of sin, now let Him lead you in every step.
Have your roots planted deep in Christ.
Grow in Him. Get your strength from Him.
Let Him make you strong in the faith
as you have been taught. Your life
should be full of thanks to Him.*
Colossians 2:6–7 nlv

Father, thank You for Jesus. And thank You for
His love for me. I believe He is Your Son who
led a perfect life then died on a cross. I trust
He has saved me from the punishment of sin.
I pray that He'll lead me every step of every
day. I want to walk in Him! I want to grow in
Him! Please help all that I think, say, and do to
be rooted and growing in Him. In Jesus' name
I pray, amen.

SAFE AND PROTECTED

The LORD will protect you from all danger;
he will keep you safe. He will protect you
as you come and go now and forever.
PSALM 121:7–8 GNT

Father, it's such a comfort to know You'll protect me from all danger. Tonight, I can go to sleep in peace knowing that You watch over my life—now and forever. You love me with a perfect love. Knowing that You watch over me and keep me safe is just part of the proof of Your love. I pray that when I'm tempted to feel scared, I'll remember Your love and protection and rest in You. Thank You for keeping me safe! Amen.

TOGETHER

*Live your lives as the Good News of Christ
says you should. If I come to you or not,
I want to hear that you are standing true
as one. I want to hear that you are working
together as one, preaching the Good News.*
PHILIPPIANS 1:27 NLV

Lord Jesus, I want to live my life like Your Word says I should. And I want to join my life with other believers so that we can work together as one for Your glory. I pray that You'll bless me with great relationships with other Christ followers. Please bring wonderful friends who love You into my life so we can help keep each other close to You. Thank You that I don't have to face this Christian walk all on my own. In Your name I pray, amen.

LEARNING TO TAKE ADVICE

Listen to what you are taught.
Be wise; do not neglect it.
PROVERBS 8:33 GNT

Father, I admit that sometimes (okay, most times!) I want to have my own way. I know what I want to do—and then I do it. I also think I know what's best for me. It's hard for me to realize that I don't always know what's best. And it's really hard to accept the fact that other people can help point me in the right direction. Even if I don't always want to listen to advice from my parents or teachers, please help me remember that they were young once too. And their experiences and advice actually can help me. Please help me not to shut them out but instead to listen to them and then make wise decisions. In Jesus' name I pray, amen.

WHAT IS TRUTH?

So Pilate asked him, "Are you a king, then?"
Jesus answered, "You say that I am a king.
I was born and came into the world for
this one purpose, to speak about the truth.
Whoever belongs to the truth listens to me."
"And what is truth?" Pilate asked.
JOHN 18:37-38 GNT

Lord, so much is confusing in today's world. And there's so much noise when people share their ideas of what's right and wrong. When I listen to what everybody says, all I hear are opinions. Not much seems to make sense. I pray that I'll know and understand Your truth and let it guide my life. In fact, help it change the decisions I make and the way I think and live. Thank You that Your Word is true. Thank You that Jesus alone is the Way, the Truth, and the Life. Amen.

WHAT AM I?

I look at your heavens, which you made with your fingers. I see the moon and stars, which you created. But why are people even important to you? Why do you take care of human beings?
PSALM 8:3-4 NCV

Creator God, I am in awe of You! You've created everything! When I look around and see the sunrise and sunset, it's obvious that You are the ultimate artist. When I see the moon and stars and think about how little I am and how humongous the universe is, I'm amazed. It's mind-boggling to think of the way You've created humans so uniquely. No one escapes Your notice. Who are we that You would do that? I may not appreciate each day, but You still care for me and provide for me. My heart is beating, and there's breath in my lungs. Thank You!

YOUR LITTLE LAMB

"I am the good shepherd. I know my sheep, and my sheep know me, just as the Father knows me, and I know the Father. I give my life for the sheep."
JOHN 10:14-15 NCV

Lord Jesus, when I think of sheep, I picture cute little fluffy animals. But as adorable as they are, sheep love to wander and get themselves into trouble. Sheep need someone to lead them and guide them to keep them safe and out of danger. And they know their shepherd's voice so well and listen only to him. Just like those sweet but stupid sheep, I need You to lead me and guide me. Please keep me safe and out of danger. I pray that I'll know You and Your voice and listen to You. I'm Your little lamb. You are a very good Shepherd! In Your name I pray, amen.

FRIENDS FOREVER

*The LORD is the friend of those who obey him
and he affirms his covenant with them.*
PSALM 25:14 GNT

Lord, sometimes I feel so lonely. It doesn't seem
like I have any true friends. It's been easy for
me to fall into a trap of trusting in my friends
and being happy or unhappy because of them.
When I feel loved and included, life is great.
And I'm sent crashing down whenever I feel left
out. The amazing thing is, though, that You are
my Friend—my best Friend. You have promised
amazing things. For that, I'm so grateful. Even
though I don't always feel like I can measure up
to You as the kind of friend You deserve, I'm in
awe of You. Thank You for Your love and Your
kindness! You are the best Friend of all. Amen.

EVEN MORE

Finally, our friends, you learned from us how you should live in order to please God. This is, of course, the way you have been living. And now we beg and urge you in the name of the Lord Jesus to do even more.
1 THESSALONIANS 4:1 GNT

Lord Jesus, it's so tempting to live for myself every day. Only thinking about and doing what I want seems really tempting. Yet living in a way that pleases You is so much better. Deep down I do want to please You. Just because I know what I should do, though, it doesn't mean that it's easy to choose to do what pleases You. I pray that I'll please and obey You more and more, even when I don't feel like it. In Your holy name I pray, amen.

MAKE ME STRONG

Our enemies were trying to scare us,
thinking, "They will get too weak to work.
Then the wall will not be finished."
But I prayed, "God, make me strong."
NEHEMIAH 6:9 NCV

Lord, my enemies try to ruin what I do and scare me. Please help me to trust You and remember that You will take care of me. I don't have to fear anything! Please make me strong, and let me do the work You have for me. Please help me to be kind to others and show Your love. Please help me to do what's right in Your eyes, even if other people make fun of it or try to make life tough for me. You're the One I'm living for. In Jesus' name I pray, amen.

FREE AND FORGIVEN!

*For by the blood of Christ we are set free,
that is, our sins are forgiven. How great is
the grace of God, which he gave to
us in such large measure!*
EPHESIANS 1:7–8 GNT

Jesus, You are perfect, and I am so not perfect. But You chose to love me anyway. And You do so much more than love me! You gave Your very life for me so I could have a relationship with You. You bought me at a price. And You've forgiven me of my sins. I have a lot of them, and You know every single one, yet You still forgive me. As if that wasn't enough, You give me all these amazing gifts. You bless me with the undeserved riches of Your grace. I'm so unworthy but so thankful. In Your name I pray, amen.

MY HEART AT PEACE

Peace of mind means a healthy body,
but jealousy will rot your bones.
PROVERBS 14:30 NCV

Father God, I know You give peace. When my heart is calm and resting in You, I feel more alive. I'm happy and content with what I have. And when I'm not at peace? Eww. So often jealousy and envy steal my peace and take my eyes off all You've given me. I look and see what other people have and wonder why it can't be mine. The truth is, though, You've given me what's best for me. And You know so much better than I do. I pray that I will learn how to be content in any situation so I can feel Your true peace. In Jesus' name I pray, amen.

NEVER CHANGING

*Every good action and every perfect
gift is from God. These good gifts come
down from the Creator of the sun, moon,
and stars, who does not change
like their shifting shadows.*
JAMES 1:17 NCV

Father, it's amazing that You never change. You
are who You say You are. You are my rock, my
strong foundation. Everything in this world feels
like it changes. But You stay the same. You'll
never leave me. Thank You for being the One I
can completely trust. And thank You for giving
me good and perfect gifts. You know just what I
need when I need it—and You generously give
to me. Every good and perfect gift comes from
You. You are so very good to me, and I love
You! Amen.

SUCH A TIME AS THIS

"Yet who knows—maybe it was for a time like this that you were made queen!"
ESTHER 4:14 GNT

Father, I know I should be glad right where I am now. Amazingly, You've chosen this exact time and place in history for me. You know this is when and where I should be. Please help me keep that in mind when I'd rather speed up time. Sometimes I'd rather fast-forward. What will I be like as a teenager? Or a woman? What will I do? Will I get married and have children? Where will I live? I have so many questions, and I'd love to know the answers. But for now, I need to wait for You and Your timing. In my waiting, please help me enjoy everything You're giving me right now. In Jesus' name I pray, amen.

GOOD TIMES!

As the scripture says, "If you want to enjoy life and wish to see good times, you must keep from speaking evil and stop telling lies."
1 PETER 3:10 GNT

Lord Jesus, I'd love to see good times! And the thought of loving my life is fantastic. But I don't always realize that what I say has so much to do with a good life. It's hard to remember that my words have the power to change everything. But they do! Please help me remember that what I choose to say—or not say—makes a huge difference. And please keep my tongue from evil and my lips from telling lies. I don't want to be two-faced, and I don't want to be a liar. I also don't want to say things that hurt others or bring shame to You. Amen.

COURAGE

The LORD has shown me, Ezra, his love in the presence of the king, those who advise the king, and the royal officers. Because the LORD my God was helping me, I had courage, and I gathered the leaders of Israel to return with me.
EZRA 7:28 NCV

Lord, thank You for filling the Bible with stories of real, ordinary men and women who did amazing things for You. In the book of Ezra, You show how one man—Ezra—made a huge difference. He made that difference because You were helping Him. He didn't have to fear the king, and He didn't have to fear leading the Israelites, because You led Him. And he courageously followed You. I pray that You'll give me courage to do what You want me to do. In Jesus' name I pray, amen.

FOCUS

*You have been raised to life with Christ,
so set your hearts on the things that are
in heaven, where Christ sits on his
throne at the right side of God.*
COLOSSIANS 3:1 GNT

Father, thank You for Jesus! Thank You for His perfect life and how He willingly paid for my sins. And thank You for raising me to life with Him! It's easy to focus on myself and the things of this world, but I pray that You'll help me seek things that are above. Please take my focus off of myself. I don't want to selfishly think about me, me, me all the time. Instead, set my mind and my heart on You. I pray that I won't get bogged down with things that other people think are so important—grades, clothes, belongings, relationships, or popularity. But help me focus on You. I love You!

FOLLOWING HIS LEAD

I praise the LORD because he advises me.
Even at night, I feel his leading. I keep the
LORD before me always. Because he is
close by my side, I will not be hurt.
PSALM 16:7–8 NCV

Lord, I praise You! You are so good to me, especially in the way You guide me so lovingly and gently. Please keep leading and instructing me even while I sleep. Please help me listen to You and follow. I pray that I'll keep my eyes on You and not look to my own ways. It's hard not to chase after things I think I want. Instead, please help me choose what's right in Your eyes. Thank You for advising me and always being close by my side. I want to follow Your lead! In Jesus' name I pray, amen.

MY REASON FOR HOPE

*Let us hold on to the hope we say we have
and not be changed. We can trust God
that He will do what He promised.*
HEBREWS 10:23 NLV

Father God, I put my faith in You completely and
totally. I believe You are who You say You are. I
believe Jesus is Your perfect Son who came to
pay for my sins with His life. And I live in that
hope. I trust You, and I expect all that You've
promised will come true in Your perfect timing.
I may not know what each day will bring, but
I know that You are faithful. And You're in the
middle of weaving together something very
beautiful in and through my life. Even if things
look or feel messy right now, You can and will
make something absolutely beautiful from my
mess. Thank You!

TO HAVE A FRIEND IS
TO BE A FRIEND

*Some friends may ruin you, but a real
friend will be more loyal than a brother.*
PROVERBS 18:24 NCV

Lord God, Your Word says that a real friend
sticks closer than a brother. It also says a friend
loves at all times. That means it's so important
for me to be a good friend, not just when times
are good and I'm having a lot of fun. To be a
good friend, I need to stick with my friend in
hard times, especially heartbreaking moments.
Please help me to be the kind of friend I would
like to have. Please help me to look for and find
ways to care for my friends and make their days
better. Please help me to encourage and love
my friends well out of all the love You've given
me. In Jesus' name I pray, amen.

I LOVE YOU!

*You have not seen Christ, but still you
love him. You cannot see him now, but you
believe in him. So you are filled with a joy
that cannot be explained, a joy full of glory.*
1 PETER 1:8 NCV

Jesus, faith is a pretty exciting thing. Even
though I've never seen You, I have complete
faith in You. I know You're real. I know You're
alive. And I love You! I believe in You. And in
my faith, You fill me with joy I can't explain.
Sometimes it feels like I might explode with joy!
I pray that I'll live out my belief in You and that
my joy and peace will be contagious. Because
You love me, I want to love other people really,
really well. Thank You for saving me and filling
me with such wonderful feelings I can't explain.
Amen.

TRUSTWORTHY

*How happy is the man who has made the
Lord his trust, and has not turned to the
proud or to the followers of lies.*
PSALM 40:4 NLV

Father, I'm glad You're worthy of my trust. I'm thankful You're my God. And I'm grateful I can put my trust in You and You alone. I don't want to turn away from You. This world is filled with many people and things that are fighting for my attention and love. I don't want my heart to follow a lie. I don't want to give my time and thoughts to anything that would lead me away from You. Please help me realize what the things of this world are—and help me turn away from them. I want to keep my eyes on You and trust You completely. In Jesus' name I pray, amen.

PUTTING OTHERS FIRST

When you do things, do not let selfishness or pride be your guide. Instead, be humble and give more honor to others than to yourselves. Do not be interested only in your own life, but be interested in the lives of others.
PHILIPPIANS 2:3-4 NCV

Father, pride has a sneaky way of creeping into my thoughts. I think I'm better than I really am. I feel like I deserve so much. But if I want to live like Jesus, I need to remember that He was totally humble! He gave up everything to come to earth, and not even as a king with life in a fancy palace and a bunch of servants. No, He came to serve others. I pray that I'll stop focusing on myself. Please help me to figure out how I can help others without thinking of what could be in it for me. Amen.

DON'T BE SO ANGRY

*Don't become angry quickly,
because getting angry is foolish.*
ECCLESIASTES 7:9 NCV

Heavenly Father, sometimes I can get so angry. I know I shouldn't be this way though! And really, I don't like getting angry because I know it changes every part of me. It feels like it gets lodged in my heart and changes the way I think and speak and respond to others—and to You. I want to remember that this life is too short to waste my time getting angry. Instead, please help me find a better way to deal with my frustration, let it go, and move on. And, as hard as it may seem, please help me forgive others like You've forgiven me. Amen.

ASHAMED?

"The people who live now are living in a sinful and evil time. If people are ashamed of me and my teaching, the Son of Man will be ashamed of them when he comes with his Father's glory and with the holy angels."
MARK 8:38 NCV

Lord Jesus, tonight I hate to admit this to You. But You know everything—and I want to confess. Sometimes I'm afraid to stand up for You. When people say awful things, I'm quiet. Instead of speaking up for what is right, I don't. Could You please help me to be bolder for You, Lord? I'm not ashamed of You and Your words. At least I don't want to be. Could You please help me stand up for Your truth? And stand up for You? I want to be a good example for You in this world. I love You!

STEP BY STEP

My steps have followed Your paths.
My feet have not turned from them.
PSALM 17:5 NLV

Father God, knowing that You will direct each of my steps is a huge comfort. I pray that I'll stay to Your paths and not wander outside of Your will. As You guide me, You won't let my feet slip. I don't have to worry about stumbling and falling when I'm walking through life with You. Even if I don't know where I'm going in the future, I pray that I'll walk the path You have me on right now. I absolutely trust You know where You're taking me, and You'll walk with me every step of the way—when the road seems rough, and when it's easy. Thank You for lovingly guiding me and for having a plan for my life! Amen.

SETTING AN EXAMPLE

Do not let anyone treat you as if you
are unimportant because you are young.
Instead, be an example to the believers
with your words, your actions, your love,
your faith, and your pure life.
1 TIMOTHY 4:12 NCV

Father, in the big scope of things, I'm just a tiny dot in the big picture of eternity. But I hope You'll use me to make a difference in the world. Please help me to make my family better by being part of it. Please help me step out in faith and make my school a better place. Even if I have to try hard and not focus on myself so much, please help me make life better for people who meet me. In other words, please make my life count, even if I'm young. In Jesus' name I pray, amen.

REMEMBER THE GREAT THINGS

"Obey the LORD and serve him faithfully with all your heart. Remember the great things he has done for you."
1 SAMUEL 12:24 GNT

Lord, You have done so many great things for me! Tonight, as I fall asleep, I want to remember all of the ways You are so good to me and what amazing experiences and people You've brought into my life. Thank You! When I think back to what You've done for me today, thank You for all of Your good gifts. I pray that I'll obey You. And I pray that I'll serve You faithfully with all of my heart for all of my days. You are such a good, good God! Amen.

GUARANTEED

The truth is the Good News. When you heard the truth, you put your trust in Christ. Then God marked you by giving you His Holy Spirit as a promise. The Holy Spirit was given to us as a promise that we will receive everything God has for us. God's Spirit will be with us until God finishes His work of making us complete.

Ephesians 1:13–14 nlv

Lord, thank You for Your Good News! Thank You that Your Holy Spirit guarantees my future with You. It might be a while until I see You in heaven, but until then Your Spirit is proof that I'm Yours. I've been saved by trusting in Jesus. And I've been protected through the promise of Your Spirit. Thank You for Jesus! Thank You for the way Your Holy Spirit guarantees my future with You. And thank You for making me complete. Amen.

A SOFT HEART

He said, "Go, and tell these people, 'You hear
and hear but do not understand. You look and
look but do not see.' Make the hearts of these
people hard. May their ears hear little and
their eyes see little. Or they will see with
their eyes and hear with their ears
and understand with their hearts,
and turn again and be healed."
ISAIAH 6:9–10 NLV

Father, You can shut ears, close eyes, and make
hearts hard. I pray this won't happen to me! If
I turn from You, my heart will get harder until
I just won't hear or see You at work. But I want
to hear and understand You. I want to see and
recognize You. Please keep my heart tender
to Your leading. Shape me into a girl who is
quick to listen and obey. I want to see with my
eyes, hear with my ears, and understand with
my heart. Amen.

COME WITH TRUST

*Let us go with complete trust to the throne
of God. We will receive His loving-kindness
and have His loving-favor to help
us whenever we need it.*

HEBREWS 4:16 NLV

Father, so often I feel like I need to come to You with my act all together. But because I feel like a hot mess and like I'm so far from perfect, sometimes I feel like I can't come to You. Yet You've promised that I can come to You with complete trust. You have a throne of grace. And when I come near to You, You'll lavish me with undeserved but endless kindness, favor, and love. That kind of mercy and grace will help me when I need it the most. I pray that You'll bless me with joy and peace tonight as I rest and hope in You. I love You!

SCHOOL STRUGGLES

The lazy will not get what they want,
but those who work hard will.
PROVERBS 13:4 NCV

Father, I'm glad I can come to You at any time with anything. Lately I've felt pretty frustrated with a subject at school. I want to do great, but I don't know what to change or how exactly to improve. Please help me! Please help things make sense. Help me find the strength and determination to work as hard as I can. I want to work for You and You alone. Please help me forget about the pressure to succeed. Please help me not to focus on pleasing any teacher or my parents or even myself. But I pray that even when this class feels so difficult and confusing, You'll help me focus on working hard to glorify You—and not give up. In Jesus' name I pray, amen.

NOT EVEN ONE

As the Scriptures say: "There is no one who always does what is right, not even one. There is no one who understands. There is no one who looks to God for help. All have turned away. Together, everyone has become useless. There is no one who does anything good; there is not even one."

ROMANS 3:10–12 NCV

Father, why do people turn away from You? Why don't people seek You? I don't want to be like everyone else! On my own, I'm imperfect. As much as I try not to sin, perfection is nothing I could accomplish on my own. I can't even do what's right on my own. Perfection is in Jesus, and it's to Him I turn. I don't want to turn away, and I don't want to be useless. Through Jesus, could You please help me do what's right? In His name I pray, amen.

KEEP YOUR WAY PURE

How can a young person live a pure life?
By obeying your word. With all my
heart I try to obey you. Don't let
me break your commands.
PSALM 119:9–10 NCV

Father, it's so hard to know what is right—and then choose to do it. Please help me know what pleases You. Help me seek it out in Your Word and then live by it. And please keep my feet on the path of purity. I do seek You with all of my heart. I want to follow Your commands. There is a right way and a wrong way to live. And there is a path of purity and a path of impurity. Please help me stay on the obedient, right way. Amen.

WHY WORRY?

"So do not worry about tomorrow; it will have enough worries of its own. There is no need to add to the troubles each day brings."
MATTHEW 6:34 GNT

Father God, I believe in Your Word. I believe it's true. And I desperately need to remember and choose to believe its truth tonight. Lord, I'm nervous about tomorrow. I know Your Word tells me I don't have to worry about tomorrow. But I'm really tempted to obsess and worry about things. When I think about everything that could or might happen, please help me stick to the facts of what's really real—not live in what-ifs. And when I start feeling stressed, please help me take a deep breath and relax. Thank You that I'm able to trust in You completely! Amen.

TOSSING AND TURNING

When I lie down to sleep, the hours drag;
I toss all night and long for dawn.
JOB 7:4 GNT

Father, I haven't been sleeping well lately. I just can't fall asleep! And when I do, my sleep isn't very restful. I wake up all night long and toss and turn until it's morning. Father, please search my mind. Is anything bothering me? Do I need to confess to You anything I've done wrong lately? Am I afraid of something? If so, please help me think of it and then trust that You'll take care of it. I want to trust You completely! Please bring me peace and sleep. In Jesus' name I pray, amen.

PAY BACK?

Be sure that no one pays back wrong for wrong, but always try to do what is good for each other and for all people.
1 THESSALONIANS 5:15 NCV

Lord Jesus, living for You can seem so tough. Sometimes I selfishly want to do what I think is right for me. And when people treat me badly, I'm tempted to figure out a way I could get back at them. But I'm Your child! And You live in me. Because of that, I don't have to pay back wrong for any wrong done to me. I can choose to forgive other people and treat them with kindness. I pray that I'll do what's good for other people. Please help me look past myself and find ways to help other people out of my love for You. Please help me to be a good example for You! Amen.

TURNING MY ENEMIES TO FRIENDS

When the ways of a man are pleasing to the Lord, He makes even those who hate him to be at peace with him.
PROVERBS 16:7 NLV

Thank You for Your gift of peace, Father! I'm amazed that You have the power to change relationships. It feels like it's impossible for me to make peace with someone who's mad at me or just doesn't like me. But You make things right. You even cause my enemies to be at peace with me. With my whole heart I ask that You'll be happy with what I say and do. I pray that everything I do will please You. In Jesus' name I pray, amen.

NO REGRETS

The kind of sorrow God wants makes
people change their hearts and lives.
This leads to salvation, and you cannot
be sorry for that. But the kind of
sorrow the world has brings death.
2 Corinthians 7:10 ncv

Father God, sometimes it's easy to live with regrets. Choices I make seem so wrong. Sometimes I can't believe the things I say or do! Can You please help me? I'd love to make choices that honor You. Those choices will help me live without regrets. When I'm tempted to react in anger, help me choose what pleases You. I pray I'll be able to live tomorrow without regrets. If and when I do make a bad choice, please help me quickly realize it and change—not continue in my sin and add to my trouble. Please guide me. I want to follow You! In Jesus' name I pray, amen.

DOING A U-TURN

"So I will judge you, O people of Israel, each of you by what he has done," says the Lord God. "Be sorry for all your sins and turn away from them, so sin will not destroy you."
EZEKIEL 18:30 NLV

Father, I have sinned. I can call it a mistake or messing up or a bad choice, but the truth is I sinned. Today I gave in to temptation, and I'm feeling ashamed and unworthy. Please forgive me. I want to repent—not just ask for forgiveness, but truly change and turn from my sin. Like a car doing a U-turn, I want to turn from my sin and go in the other direction toward right choices. Thank You, Lord, for forgiveness through Jesus that I don't deserve—and favor I never could earn on my own. In Jesus' name I pray, amen.

CHOSEN

*God has chosen you. You are holy and loved
by Him. Because of this, your new life should
be full of loving-pity. You should be kind to
others and have no pride. Be gentle
and be willing to wait for others.*
COLOSSIANS 3:12 NLV

Father, You've chosen me! Each time I'm
tempted to listen to voices that tell me I'm
not wanted, accepted, or good enough, please
remind me that You, the holy God of the universe, chose me. Help me live like I've been
chosen by You. Please help me to be kind. I
admit there are plenty of people in this world
I'd rather not be kind to, but I know that kindness is possible through You. Guard me from
thinking more highly of myself than I should.
Instead, please help me treat others as You'd
like—humbly with patience, kindness, and
gentleness. Amen.

TRUST AND OBEY

My Christian friends, you have obeyed me when I was with you. You have obeyed even more when I have been away. You must keep on working to show you have been saved from the punishment of sin. Be afraid that you may not please God. He is working in you. God is helping you obey Him. God is doing what He wants done in you.
PHILIPPIANS 2:12-13 NLV

Father God, I want to obey You! As hard as it may seem, when I feel like I want to do my own thing and live my life my own way, I do want to trust You and obey. Please help me remember that as I keep You as Lord of my life, You'll direct my path. It's amazing that You have a good purpose for me and that You'll work to make it happen. Thanks for choosing to use me! Amen.

NOTHING

For I know that nothing can keep us from the love of God. Death cannot! Life cannot! Angels cannot! Leaders cannot! Any other power cannot! Hard things now or in the future cannot! The world above or the world below cannot! Any other living thing cannot keep us away from the love of God which is ours through Christ Jesus our Lord.
ROMANS 8:38–39 NLV

Lord Jesus, the fact that absolutely nothing can or will separate me from the love of God that is in You is so amazing. Nothing will separate me from the love found in You! Nothing in this life. Not even death. Nothing I did in my past or am doing right now. Nothing I'll do in the future. I'm completely safe in Your love. My safety in You will help me sleep sweetly, resting in You tonight. I love You!

WORDS AND THOUGHTS

Let the words of my mouth and the thoughts
of my heart be pleasing in Your eyes, O Lord,
my Rock and the One Who saves me.
PSALM 19:14 NLV

Father, lately I've been obsessing over something. I can't stop thinking about it. At all. Obsessing so much that it could be considered an idol. Could You please help me change my thinking? I want to keep my focus on You. I'd like what my heart dwells on to be acceptable in Your sight—and that means not being consumed by the thoughts and worries of this world. As hard as it may be to change my thinking or my words, I want to do it. Please help me! In Jesus' name I pray, amen.

READY

*Get your minds ready for good use.
Keep awake. Set your hope now and
forever on the loving-favor to be given
you when Jesus Christ comes again.*
1 PETER 1:13 NLV

Lord Jesus, this world isn't an easy place to live in. You know that—that's why You came to save me. As I drift off to sleep, I pray that You'll get my mind ready for action and good use when I start a new day tomorrow. Please help me remember that I can't just drift through life. I need to protect my heart. I need to put my mind in gear. When I'm tempted to go my own way, please bring me back to You. Instead of floating along and accepting whatever comes my way, I need to make decisions that point to You and Your goodness in my life. In Your name I pray, amen.

CREATED BY YOU

*I praise you because you made me in an
amazing and wonderful way. What you have
done is wonderful. I know this very well.*
PSALM 139:14 NCV

Lord God, Your Word tells me that I'm wonderfully made. I'm grateful for that truth, but I
don't always believe it. I don't always like the
way I look. Some days I don't like my hair. Other
days it's my face. And I wish my body were
different. Yet You made me just the way I am.
As the master artist, You believe I'm beautiful.
You created me to look like this for a specific
reason. When I'm tempted to be unhappy with
the way I look, please help me remember that
You see me, You know me, and You love me—just
the way I am. In Jesus' name I pray, amen.

GOD IS FOR YOU!

If God is for us, who can be against us?
ROMANS 8:31 GNT

Father God, it's so good to be known and loved by You. I absolutely adore knowing that You are *for* me. When You are for me, no one else can be against me. Oh, sure, it doesn't always seem like everyone likes me (and not all people do), but when it comes down to it, You're in control of everything. You can and do change people's hearts. And You can and do change situations. I want to boldly trust You and live out my faith, knowing that I can be a brave girl and follow Your leading all my life. Thank You for the amazing way You care for me! Amen.

I NEED YOU!

*Listen to my prayer, O Lord, and hear
my cry for help! When I am in trouble,
don't turn away from me! Listen to me,
and answer me quickly when I call!*
PSALM 102:1–2 GNT

Lord, I need You! I don't feel like I can handle things on my own. I'm nervous and scared. I know You can help me though. Deep down I know You'll never leave me. Please help me trust that. When it feels like my life is out of control and I don't have any hope, I want to remember You. You're full of love. You listen to the cries of my heart. You care about how I'm feeling right now. And You know me. Please fill me with Your peace and help me know that You've heard my cries for help. In Jesus' name I pray, amen.

ALIVE!

But God had so much loving-kindness.
He loved us with such a great love. Even when
we were dead because of our sins, He made
us alive by what Christ did for us. You have
been saved from the punishment
of sin by His loving-favor.
EPHESIANS 2:4–5 NLV

Father! You are so absolutely rich with Your loving-kindness. And I don't deserve it. Thank You for saving me from the punishment I deserve. Thank You for making me alive through Christ! Thank You for loving me so much, even when I was far from You. Tonight, when I think about all that's happened in my day, I thank You that I can take time to think about what really matters: Your love brings me to life. Even when details of my life crowd out what's important, I can appreciate You and Your great gifts to me. Thank You!

WHAT'S MY PURPOSE?

*The Lord will finish the work He started
for me. O Lord, Your loving-kindness
lasts forever. Do not turn away
from the works of Your hands.*

PSALM 138:8 NLV

Lord, I wonder what I should do with my life.
What have I been created for? Why am I here?
Why did You put me right here, right now? Even
though I have a zillion questions, You have a
zillion answers. You know why I'm here. You
know what I've been created for. You know
Your purpose for me—and You know how I can
fulfill that. I pray that I'll follow Your leading. I
pray that You'll reveal Your purpose for me and
reassure me through the circumstances of my
life. Thank You for creating me with a specific
purpose. This is huge to try to comprehend and
so exciting! In Jesus' name I pray, amen.

ENCOURAGING AND HELPING

*And so encourage one another and help
one another, just as you are now doing.*
1 THESSALONIANS 5:11 GNT

Lord, sometimes I say things I don't want to say or do things I don't want to do. I don't usually like what I think or say when I'm in a bad mood. I don't know how to change, but I want to be a bright spot in the world. When I'm tempted to tear people down in my grumpiness, please help me change to words that build people up. When I'd rather disrespect my parents because they don't understand what I'm going through, please help me honor them with the words I say and my body language too. When I'd love to use a hurtful comeback, please shut the door of my mouth. Please change my moods, words, thoughts, and actions so they please You. Amen.

TAMING MY TONGUE

Those who are sure of themselves do not talk all the time. People who stay calm have real insight.
PROVERBS 17:27 GNT

Lord Jesus, sometimes I wonder if it matters what I say. Are words really that important? Then I remember that *You* are the Word made flesh. You matter. And what You said matters. That means what I say matters too. Please help me watch what I say! When I'm tempted to blurt out every single thought that comes to mind, please help me control my tongue. Before I share absolutely everything I want to say, please help me remember that I can and should honor You with my words. When I'd love to talk about every single detail and every single opinion I have about people or places or things, please help me to stop and think before I speak. In Your name I pray, amen.

DO YOU BELIEVE THIS?

Jesus said to her, "I am the One Who raises the dead and gives them life. Anyone who puts his trust in Me will live again, even if he dies. Anyone who lives and has put his trust in Me will never die. Do you believe this?"
JOHN 11:25-26 NLV

Jesus, I believe You do raise the dead and give life! I'm thankful that You came to earth so people like me *can* believe in You and never die. And I'm thankful that all I need is to believe. I don't have to jump through a lot of hoops or worry about doing a bunch of good things to earn my way to forever life with You. Trust in You can be something so simple yet hard to actually do. But tonight I want to tell You that I do trust in You. I love You!

SWEET SLEEP

It is useless to work so hard for a living,
getting up early and going to bed late.
For the LORD provides for those he
loves, while they are asleep.
PSALM 127:2 GNT

Lord, I'm having such a hard time falling asleep tonight. When I toss and turn, it feels like I can't turn my brain off. I can't seem to stop thinking about what happened today or what could be coming in the future. It feels like my thoughts are taken over by worry. Would You please quiet my thoughts? I pray that You'll grant me peace as only You can. And in that peace, please give me rest. Please help me rest peacefully tonight so I can wake up refreshed tomorrow morning, ready to live for You. In Jesus' name I pray, amen.

COME NEAR

*Come near to God, and God will come near
to you. You sinners, clean sin out of your
lives. You who are trying to follow
God and the world at the same
time, make your thinking pure.*
JAMES 4:8 NCV

Father, I'm sorry I get distracted by things of
this world. Please forgive me. I want to come
near to You. I wish I could cuddle up close to
You and know You're there. Tonight, please fill
my heart with Your peace and love. I love You
and want to be able to shut out all the noise
from this world and focus on You alone. In my
heart of hearts, I know You've given me all of
Yourself through Your Son. But how much of me
do You have? Please help me not to be afraid
to give You all of myself. Amen.

WHERE ARE YOU?

During the day I call to you, my God,
but you do not answer; I call at
night, but get no rest.
PSALM 22:2 GNT

Father, I want to hear from You! Sometimes when I pray, it seems like my prayers are just bouncing back to me—like You don't hear them. Deep down, though, I know You hear. And deep down I know You care. Still, I sometimes get discouraged waiting for an answer from You. I pray that I'll continue to trust in You even when it doesn't feel like You're there. Would You please give me peace as I trust and wait? Morning and night and all throughout the day, I want to tell You what I'm feeling. Please help my faith grow stronger and stronger as I wait for You. In Jesus' name I pray, amen.

LET MY LIGHT SHINE

"You are the light of the world. You cannot hide a city that is on a mountain. Men do not light a lamp and put it under a basket. They put it on a table so it gives light to all in the house. Let your light shine in front of men. Then they will see the good things you do and will honor your Father Who is in heaven."

MATTHEW 5:14-16 NLV

Lord Jesus, I pray that You'll use me as a light wherever I go. In school, at church, in my community, in my home, with my friends, and with strangers—please help me faithfully stand up for what I believe in and what is true. Let my light drive away darkness and shine in this world! Please help me to live for You! In Your name I pray, amen.

LOOKING FORWARD WITH JOY

She is strong and is respected by the people.
She looks forward to the future with joy.
PROVERBS 31:25 NCV

Father, because I trust in You, I don't have to worry about my future. In fact, I can look forward to the future with joy! When people around me are stressed out by what's going on in the world or are so worried about what they should do, I can rest in You. You give me strength. And as I trust in You completely, I become stronger. Thank You! Knowing that I don't have to fear what's coming is huge. And feeling the strength You give me is such a comfort. You are good to me, and I'll always be grateful. Amen.

MORE IMPORTANT

*"Are not two small birds sold for a very small
piece of money? And yet not one of the birds
falls to the earth without your Father knowing
it. God knows how many hairs you have
on your head. So do not be afraid. You are
more important than many small birds."*
MATTHEW 10:29–31 NLV

Father, You are the Creator of all life. I'm one girl
out of so many other girls—they seem countless
to me, yet You know exactly how many girls
You've ever created. And not just each girl,
but You know how many strands of hair are on
every head. The fact that You are all-knowing
is awesome and amazing. It's also a little scary!
Not only do You know me so well, but You also
love me and believe I'm important. Thank You.
You are a good, good God!

DARK IS LIGHT

I could ask the darkness to hide me or the light around me to turn into night, but even darkness is not dark for you, and the night is as bright as the day. Darkness and light are the same to you.

PSALM 139:11–12 GNT

Lord God, nothing about this world is above or beyond You. You created the light and the darkness. So even though darkness is so overwhelming and scary to me, it's not even dark to You. As much as I can't understand it, darkness is like light to You. The night shines like day. Because of that, I can fall asleep tonight in peace. I don't have to worry about what I can't see in the darkness, because You can see everything—and You're right here to protect me. Amen.

WHATEVER YOU DO

Whatever you say or do, do it in the name of the Lord Jesus. Give thanks to God the Father through the Lord Jesus.
COLOSSIANS 3:17 NLV

Father, I want to honor You in everything I say and do—and I want people to see Jesus living in me. But it isn't always easy. In fact, it's easy to forget that I need to watch what I say. If You need to, Lord, please keep a door over my mouth. . .and shut it! If that's what it takes to keep me from saying things that don't bring You honor, then I'm willing. Thank You for the voice You've given me. Please help me to use it to share Your love and kindness. And thank You that I can do things for You. Please use me to reach this world for You! Amen.

A NEW THING

The LORD says, "Forget what happened
before, and do not think about the past.
Look at the new thing I am going to do.
It is already happening. Don't you see it?"
<small>ISAIAH 43:18-19 NCV</small>

I praise You for being God Almighty, full of
power. I know I should try to be content with
where You have me in life, Lord, because You
do have a purpose and a plan! But sometimes
I wish I could have a fresh start. I feel stuck
right now, but I trust that someday You'll bring
changes into my life. When those changes do
come and I realize I have a new beginning,
please help me remember where I've come
from. I pray that I won't focus on the past, but
I don't want to forget what You've done in my
life. In Jesus' name I pray, amen.

SHINE LIKE STARS

Do everything without complaining or arguing, so that you may be innocent and pure as God's perfect children, who live in a world of corrupt and sinful people. You must shine among them like stars lighting up the sky, as you offer them the message of life.
PHILIPPIANS 2:14–16 GNT

Father, I confess it's really easy to grumble and complain. But when I do, I end up looking for what's wrong or annoying, and I shut my eyes to what's really good. I miss out on Your good gifts when all I do is find fault with things and argue. I want to be innocent and pure in this world. I want to live like Your child and shine like a star in the sky! I need to hold on to Your message of life and let that shine through what I say, do, and think. Amen.

YOU ARE MY TRUST

LORD, you are my hope. LORD,
I have trusted you since I was young.
PSALM 71:5 NCV

Lord, sometimes I wonder how I can trust You. But then the bigger question is this: How could I *not* trust You? You're completely worthy of my trust. With hope, I know You and Your promises are true. What would my life be like without You? I'm thankful I've known You as a girl. I want to love, trust, and follow You the rest of my life! Who or what would I trust in if it wasn't for You? Thank You for keeping Your promises and being trustworthy. Amen.

FOLLOWING YOU

Because Abraham had faith, he obeyed
God when God called him to leave his home.
He was to go to another country that God
promised to give him. He left his home
without knowing where he was going.
HEBREWS 11:8 NLV

Father God, You are close to those who are faithful to You. You asked Abraham, in the book of Genesis, to do a huge thing—trust You by leaving His home and following You. Instead of setting his heart on what he knew or what was comfy, he chose to obey You. He had no idea where You would lead him. He only knew that You *would* lead him. Just like Abraham, I pray that I'll be ready and willing to follow where You'll lead me, even when it seems scary. I want to follow You! Amen.

MY POWERFUL GOD

*"Now all the people of the earth may know
that the hand of the Lord is powerful, so that
you may fear the Lord your God forever."*
JOSHUA 4:24 NLV

Father God, You always protect and provide
for Your children. Your hand has worked so
powerfully in the lives of people who believe
in You, including mine. I know the great things
You have done for me—things I never could
have done for myself. You've treated me with
so much kindness and favor. Thank You! I want
to remember the way You've so faithfully and
lovingly provided for me. You are full of power.
You always have been and You always will be.
With You as my Lord and my God, who on earth
should I fear? In Jesus' name I pray, amen.

WALKING IN THE LIGHT

*If we live in the light as He is in the light,
we share what we have in God with
each other. And the blood of Jesus Christ,
His Son, makes our lives clean from all sin.*
1 JOHN 1:7 NLV

Father, I know what it's like to be scared of the dark. Nighttime can be spooky just because I can't see what's out in the dark. When I was younger, the darkness seemed even more threatening; nightlights and flashlights were helpful because the light drove away darkness. Just as the dark of night is less scary when there's light, it's much easier to walk through my life with Your light. I am so thankful Jesus is the Light of the World. I'm thankful I know Him. I'm thankful for the way Your Word is a lamp to my feet and a light for my path. And I'm thankful I don't have to stumble through the darkness of the world on my own, but that You light the way. I do want to walk in Your light! In Jesus' name I pray, amen.

WISHING AND HOPING

People can make all kinds of plans,
but only the LORD's plan will happen.
PROVERBS 19:21 NCV

Father God, You know that I have many dreams for my future and even some plans that I hope will make my wishes a reality. I know what I'd like to have happen in my life. But really, Your plan is what will happen. You have plans for me and things that I need to experience. I want to trust You! Please help me welcome Your plans for me. If I need to change my hopes and dreams to go along with Your purpose for my life, please help me to be open to change. I'm excited to see what You'd like to do in my life and through me! Amen.

CREATED FOR GOOD WORKS

God has made us what we are. In Christ Jesus, God made us to do good works, which God planned in advance for us to live our lives doing.
Ephesians 2:10 NCV

Father, I'm blown away that You created me to do good works—and that You've already planned them for me! I really wish I could skip ahead and see what they are, but I'll try to wait patiently as You show me Your plans over time. It's amazing that You care for me so much and have a purpose for my life. Please fill me with courage and faith to follow Your lead and do all of the good works You have for me. Please use me in an amazing way! Amen.

LEAD ME

*The LORD is my shepherd; I have everything I
need. He lets me rest in fields of green grass
and leads me to quiet pools of fresh water.
He gives me new strength. He guides me
in the right paths, as he has promised.*
PSALM 23:1-3 GNT

Father, Your Word promises that Your sheep—
Your children!—will know their Shepherd's voice.
Please help my heart know Your voice. I love
Jesus. He is my Shepherd. I pray that He will
lead me and that I'll faithfully listen to Him
and follow. I'm so thankful He gives me all I
really need. Please help me remember that I
am Yours—and as long as I follow You, I won't
go astray. In Jesus' name I pray, amen.

THE MOMENT

"I am telling you the truth: those who hear my words and believe in him who sent me have eternal life. They will not be judged, but have already passed from death to life."

JOHN 5:24 GNT

Father, for You, belief is the difference between eternal life and eternal death. But I haven't always believed in You. In fact, there definitely was a time in my life when I didn't. So my very big, important question tonight is this: *Have* I believed in You? And when was the moment I chose to believe in Christ and to trust Him with my forever? If I've never said it before, Lord, I *do* believe in You! I believe You sent Jesus. And I trust my eternity to Him. I want to cross over from death to life. It's in Jesus' name I trust and pray. Amen.

CHOOSING FRIENDS

Spend time with the wise and you will become wise, but the friends of fools will suffer.
PROVERBS 13:20 NCV

Lord, I sometimes forget how important it is to choose my friends wisely. It's tempting to try to fit in with the popular crowd. But instead of focusing so much on what's on the outside, please help me to see what my "friends" really are like. Are they leading me away from You? Are they influencing me to do things that are mean or hurtful to others? As much as I want to have friends, I pray that I don't back down on what I know to be right. And I pray that I make choices that show my love for You. If my friends can't help me do that, I pray that You'll bring other friends into my life. In Jesus' name I pray, amen.

LIVING BY HIS WORD

Make every effort to give yourself to
God as the kind of person he will approve.
Be a worker who is not ashamed and who
uses the true teaching in the right way.
2 TIMOTHY 2:15 NCV

Thank You for Your Word, Lord. Thank You that it's true. I pray that I'd know and understand it better and use it in the right way. Help me find ways to learn what You say and watch the way You change my heart, my mind, and my entire life. As Your truth works in my heart, I want it to show in my life. More than anything, I want You to approve what I think and say and do. I don't want to be ashamed. Please help me live a life pleasing to You! Amen.

A TRUSTWORTHY GIRL

Gossips can't keep secrets,
but a trustworthy person can.
PROVERBS 11:13 NCV

Father God, You created all things—including my mouth and my tongue. I can use my words to tell others about You and bring healing and life, or I can use them to hurt and destroy. When I choose to open my mouth and talk *about* other people, usually it's hurtful. I pray that I'll learn to keep my mouth shut when I should. I pray that I'll become a trustworthy girl—worthy of the trust of others—and keep secrets when asked. I pray that I won't speak poorly about others but build people up with my words. And I pray that I won't ruin the trust of others by sharing what's meant for my ears only. Please help me think before I speak. In Jesus' name I pray, amen.

SOMETHING SPECIAL

You are a chosen people, royal priests,
a holy nation, a people for God's own
possession. You were chosen to tell about the
wonderful acts of God, who called you out
of darkness into his wonderful light.
1 PETER 2:9 NCV

Father, I don't understand why You chose me to be Yours, but I'm so thankful You did! Please help me remember that because of Jesus' sacrifice for me, I am royal and holy. Let me live like I am royal and holy in all that I say and do. Remind me that I am a princess—the daughter of the King of kings. Thank You for calling me out of the darkness and into Your wonderful light. Please help me to be a light to my friends and family who still are living in darkness. Amen.

THE APPLE OF YOUR EYE

Keep me as the apple of your eye; hide me in the shadow of your wings from the wicked who are out to destroy me, from my mortal enemies who surround me.
PSALM 17:8-9 NIV

Father, You are my protector. You know me and keep me safe. Thank You for hiding me in the shadow of Your wings. When I imagine how a mama bird would do anything to protect her babies, I know the same is true for You. You're always alert, always protecting me, always watching out for my best interests. Thank You. Thank You that I don't have to live in fear of what people will try to do to me. Thank You that even though enemies try to destroy me—sometimes quite literally—You're the One who protects me. In Jesus' name I pray, amen.

CHOOSE KINDNESS

This royal law is found in the Scriptures:
"Love your neighbor as you love yourself."
If you obey this law, you are doing right.
But if you treat one person as being more
important than another, you are sinning.
You are guilty of breaking God's law.

JAMES 2:8-9 NCV

Father, it breaks my heart when people say or do hurtful things to me. And other girls who purposely exclude me crush my spirit. Please help me look past the mean things people have said or done to try to hurt me. Please help me not look to them or their approval for my worth. Please help me remember that my value is in You. And please help me treat others without favoritism. I want to be kind and loving to everyone. Amen.

WITHOUT SIN

No one can say, "I am innocent;
I have never done anything wrong."
PROVERBS 20:9 NCV

Father, when I look around me, I see so much wrong in the world. There's so much sin! And people celebrate their sin. Father, it's wrong! And it grieves Your heart to know and see all the sin. You sent Jesus into this world to save all who fall short of Your perfection, if they'd just recognize Him as Lord. Thank You for sending Him. And thank You for opening my eyes and heart to accept Him and the sacrifice He made for me. Please forgive my sins and help me not to think of myself more highly than I should. I don't want to judge others when I'm just as guilty of sin in my life. Thank You for Jesus! In His name I pray, amen.

TALK ABOUT IT

Your heart should be holy and set apart for the Lord God. Always be ready to tell everyone who asks you why you believe as you do. Be gentle as you speak and show respect.
1 PETER 3:15 NLV

Lord Jesus, I want to set apart my heart for You. And I want to be ready to talk about all that You've done in my life. When people ask why I have hope or make certain choices, please help me tell about You! I don't want to scare people away from You, but I also don't want to be so shy that I keep my love for You hidden. I pray that I'll talk about You clearly while respecting whoever I'm talking with. I pray that it will feel natural to talk about You and how You've worked in my life. In Your name I pray, amen.

PURE AND INNOCENT

*Those who are pure in act and in thought,
who do not worship idols or make false
promises. The LORD will bless
them and save them; God will
declare them innocent.*
PSALM 24:4–5 GNT

Father, I confess that at times I'm tempted to think or do what's wrong. Sometimes I make promises I never intend to keep. Or I think it's okay just to fudge a little bit, peek at information I shouldn't see, or make sure things work out in my favor. To me it seems like a tiny thing, but in Your eyes, getting ahead this way is wrong. It's sinful—and I miss out on what You've called me to as Your daughter. Lord, I confess my guilt. Please forgive me. I want to do what's right in Your eyes! I want to be innocent. Amen.

MERCY!

But when the kindness and love of God our Savior was shown, he saved us because of his mercy. It was not because of good deeds we did to be right with him.
TITUS 3:4-5 NCV

Lord God, You are so kind! As much as people wonder where You are when bad things happen, I see Your kindness, goodness, and love all around me. You loved people so much that You made a way for us to be made right with You. Through Your mercy, You saved us! You knew we couldn't do enough good deeds on our own. There's nothing we can do to earn a right standing with You. All I need to do is believe and welcome Your mercy. Tonight, I do. I believe in You. And I'm thankful for the way You've saved me with plenty of forgiveness I'll never deserve. Amen.

IT'S A GOOD DAY!

When life is good, enjoy it. But when life is hard, remember: God gives good times and hard times, and no one knows what tomorrow will bring.
ECCLESIASTES 7:14 NCV

Father God, there are good days and bad days—and today I'm thankful for all of the very good things You've done. Thank You for all of the little things and best parts that happened today! For the times when I needed to trust You a little more, I'm thankful. For the moments You surprised me with Your faithfulness, I'm grateful. For the way You've poured out Your love and favor, I'm humbled. I love You, Lord, no matter what. But when You thrill me with good things, it really makes my day. Thank You!

A NEW CREATION

If anyone belongs to Christ, there is a
new creation. The old things have
gone; everything is made new!
2 CORINTHIANS 5:17 NCV

Father God, thank You for new beginnings! I love the fact that when I believed and trusted in Christ, I became a new creation. Everything that's in my past—all of the old things that kept me from You—are dead and gone. In their place, You've brought new things! And the new things are wonderful. Thank You for taking all that's old and wiping it away. Thank You for making all things new. I pray that I'll fall asleep tonight resting in this beautiful truth. I am a new creation in Christ! In His name I pray, amen.

NO SHAME

O my God, I trust in You. Do not let me
be ashamed. Do not let those
who fight against me win.
PSALM 25:2 NLV

Father, thank You for loving me no matter what. And thank You for always being with me. Tonight, I really need some time with You remembering who I am in You. I was so embarrassed today. Sometimes I don't know why I say the things I do or act the way I do. And I don't always like what happens to me. Honestly, some days and weeks I rarely do like what happens. But even in all of my embarrassment and frustration, please help me remember that You can work things for my good. You can use these uncomfortable, unwanted moments to turn me into a girl who trusts You. Thank You for that. Amen.

PEACE I CAN'T UNDERSTAND

*And God's peace, which is so great we
cannot understand it, will keep your
hearts and minds in Christ Jesus.*
PHILIPPIANS 4:7 NCV

Father, I'm glad that I can come to You at any time and be completely honest with You—because I feel so stressed out right now! I'm under so much pressure. And I want to do my best. I want things to go well. Please help me remember that I can rest in You. As I trust You with everything that's weighing me down, I pray that You'll fill me with a deep peace that I can't explain or even understand. Your peace, oh Lord, would be so wonderful right now! And to know that Your peace will guard my heart and mind brings great comfort and relief. Thank You!

PROMISE KEEPER

"God keeps every promise he makes. He is like a shield for all who seek his protection."
PROVERBS 30:5 GNT

Father God, thank You for Your Word. Thank You that it's true. Thank You that it's flawless. Thank You that it's timeless. I love the way it leads me. Thank You for keeping every promise You've made! Help me stay firmly grounded in You and Your Word instead of relying on worldly beliefs that are popular right now. You give me so much protection. You are my shield, and Your Word is the sword of the Spirit—the weapon I can use to defend myself every day. I pray that I'll hide Your Word in my heart and let it change my life. Amen.

HOLY AND WITHOUT BLAME

Even before the world was made,
God chose us for Himself because of His love.
He planned that we should be holy and
without blame as He sees us.

EPHESIANS 1:4 NLV

Father God, I'm amazed that You would choose me before You even created the world. Me! I'm chosen! It's something that seems so strange—yet I'm forever thankful for that. Thank You for adopting me and making me a part of Your family. Thank You for Your undeserved favor. You are so kind! I can do nothing that would make me deserve being holy and without blame as You see me, so I come to You tonight to thank You. Thank You for treating me in a way I can't begin to comprehend or deserve. I love You!

SO LONELY

I lie awake. And I feel like
a bird alone on the roof.
PSALM 102:7 NLV

Father, thank You for always being with me. I know You are. But sometimes it's so hard to keep that in mind because I'm lonely. I try to fill my loneliness with other things like friends, food, shopping, belongings, social media approval, being busy with activities, or working hard to get good grades. But only You can fill the emptiness I feel. Even if I don't always know exactly what I feel, only You can satisfy what I'm missing. I pray that I can rest in that, especially when I'm feeling alone. In Jesus' strong name I pray, amen.

FORGIVEN

*If we tell Him our sins, He is faithful and we
can depend on Him to forgive us of our sins.
He will make our lives clean from all sin.*
1 JOHN 1:9 NLV

Father God, I come to You tonight knowing
how I've sinned against You today. Of course,
I'm never perfect, because everyone sins, and
no one deserves Your glory. But I know there's
forgiveness in You. I just have to confess how
I've sinned. And so I do. Please search my heart.
And please forgive me for _____. I pray
that I won't fall into that same trap tomorrow.
Please help me make right choices. Please help
me turn away from that sin. Thank You for being
faithful and just. And Lord, thank You so much
for Your forgiveness! I don't deserve it, but I'm
very thankful for it. Amen.

WHO WILL YOU SERVE?

*"So fear the Lord. Serve Him in faith and
truth.... If you think it is wrong to serve the
Lord, choose today whom you will serve.
Choose the gods your fathers worshiped
on the other side of the river, or choose
the gods of the Amorites in whose land
you are living. But as for me and my
family, we will serve the Lord."*
JOSHUA 24:14–15 NLV

Father God, most days I want to make my own
decisions instead of being told what to do. I
want some freedom to figure out who I really am.
Please help me make choices that will glorify
You and bring You honor. I choose to serve You.
As long as I do that, I don't have to be afraid.
And I'll know You can use my independence
and choices for You. In Jesus' name I pray, amen.

TRANSFORMED!

Do not be shaped by this world; instead be changed within by a new way of thinking. Then you will be able to decide what God wants for you; you will know what is good and pleasing to him and what is perfect.
ROMANS 12:2 NCV

Father, the desires and goals of this world are so different from You and Your will. I pray that I won't try to shove myself into the mold of what's "normal" in the world. Things in this world are so imperfect! Instead, I pray that You'll change me. Please shape my mind so I can determine what Your will is. I want to do Your will because it's good, pleasing, and perfect. I pray that I'll carefully judge my options every day and choose to honor and please You with what I do and say. In Jesus' name I pray, amen.

WHY DO I NEED TO BE CORRECTED?

People who listen when they are corrected will live, but those who will not admit that they are wrong are in danger.
PROVERBS 10:17 GNT

Father, I have to admit to You that discipline and correction don't seem so great to me. When I think of discipline, I think of something I've done wrong—or some sort of set of rules I need to strictly follow. But if I would stop thinking about how much I don't like the thought of being corrected and just pay attention to what You ask of me, my life would be better! Deep down I know You correct and discipline me because You love me and want what's best for me. Please help me remember this and listen to Your direction. Amen.

MY IMPERFECT BEST

Whatever you do, work at it with all your heart, as though you were working for the Lord and not for people.
COLOSSIANS 3:23 GNT

Lord Jesus, it's an honor to serve You! I pray that every day I'll wake up and remember that I'm here to work for You—not for my parents, not for my teachers, not for a coach. But in all that I do, I want to do my best. Even if I can't be perfect, I pray that I'll still do things with all my heart—whether it's my schoolwork, or hobbies, or chores, or even the way I spend time with people around me. Serving You is an honor and a gift, and I pray that I'll think of everything I do as working for You. Amen.

MY LIGHT

The LORD is my light and the one who saves me. So why should I fear anyone? The LORD protects my life. So why should I be afraid?
PSALM 27:1 NCV

Jesus, when You came to earth, You called Yourself the Light of the World. That's exactly what You are! You light my way in this dark world. Just thinking of You and how much You love me lights my darkest days. Because of You, I don't have to fear anything or anyone. You have saved me. You brighten my darkness. And I can trust You absolutely and completely with all of me. When the worries of this world seem to pile up, I pray for Your peace to flood my heart. Please help me remember that I don't need to fear anything or anyone. You light my way. You've saved me. Thank You!

GROWING UP

We are to hold to the truth with love in our hearts. We are to grow up and be more like Christ. He is the leader of the church.
EPHESIANS 4:15 NLV

Father, thank You for drawing me close to You before I'm an adult! Even though it feels like it might take a long time until I'm on my own, I know I've grown up pretty quickly so far. Please help me remember that You'll always be my Abba Father—my Daddy! Also, please give me courage to grow up in You and be more like Christ. I want to know You more and more every day and become a teenager and a woman whose entire heart is set on You. And I want to hold on to Your truth in my heart with lots and lots of love. Amen.

ALWAYS WITH ME

God, your thoughts are precious to me.
They are so many! If I could count them,
they would be more than all the grains of
sand. When I wake up, I am still with you.
PSALM 139:17–18 NCV

Father God, I'm truly amazed by You. You are so much bigger and more powerful than anything I can imagine or understand. And Your thoughts—You know all things! The things You think and plan and bring into action are so much more than I can understand. I praise You for being all-knowing and always present. Thank You for never sleeping and never letting me out of Your thoughts. No matter what I do—whether I'm sleeping or awake—I'm with You. You'll never leave me. That is such a comfort! In Jesus' name I pray, amen.

THREE STUMBLING BLOCKS

These are the ways of the world: wanting to please our sinful selves, wanting the sinful things we see, and being too proud of what we have. None of these come from the Father, but all of them come from the world. The world and everything that people want in it are passing away, but the person who does what God wants lives forever.

1 JOHN 2:16–17 NCV

Father, it's really easy to be swayed by what's in the world. I want to please myself, I want the things I see, and I'm too proud of what I have. I get stuck thinking about those things all the time! Please help me remember that none of that is important. In fact, everything apart from You eventually will vanish. But doing what You want lasts forever. In Jesus' name I pray, amen.

SHOW ME THE WAY

The Lord Who bought you and saves you,
the Holy One of Israel, says, "I am the Lord
your God, Who teaches you to do well,
Who leads you in the way you should go."
ISAIAH 48:17 NLV

Lord, I love that You have a plan—not just for the world, but for me and my life too! Knowing that You have a plan for my future helps me rest in You. Sometimes I get scared I'm not doing the right things, or I'm confused when I need to make wise choices that affect my life. I want to pay attention to Your commands and do Your will. I want to do all that You have planned for me! Please give me opportunities, strength, and courage to do all You call me to do. And lead me in the way I should go. Amen.

NO FEAR IN DEATH

He died as we must die. Through His death He destroyed the power of the devil who has the power of death. Jesus did this to make us free from the fear of death. We no longer need to be chained to this fear.

HEBREWS 2:14–15 NLV

Father God, death is so awful. When someone close to me dies, it feels like my heart is breaking. I want to talk to them, to see them, to hug them, but I can't. You thought death was so awful that You made a way out so death doesn't need to be feared. Because You sent Jesus to earth as a man, His death and resurrection broke death's power. Thank You that for those who believe in Your Son, there's life after death. There's hope! In Jesus' precious name I pray, amen.

YOU DESERVE PRAISE!

I will praise you every day; I will praise you forever and ever. The LORD is great and worthy of our praise; no one can understand how great he is.

<small>PSALM 145:2-3 NCV</small>

Lord God, You are great! You're so worthy of praise, and I'll never know just how great You are. Tonight, I praise Your name. Thank You for all You've done in my life and heart today. Even when I think of the challenges and disappointments I faced, You were there. As I think about the wonderful moments You brought into my life today, You were there. You are faithful. You are good. And I'm thankful You've chosen me as Your daughter. When I'm tempted to focus on myself or on things of this world, please shift my focus to You and Your greatness. In Your holy name I pray, amen.

MAKING FUTURE PLANS

Listen! You who say, "Today or tomorrow we will go to this city and stay a year and make money." You do not know about tomorrow. What is your life? It is like fog. You see it and soon it is gone. What you should say is, "If the Lord wants us to, we will live and do this or that."
JAMES 4:13–15 NLV

Father, I like to try to plan ahead. I'd love to know what will happen in my future. It's fun to imagine and prepare for what might happen to me. But I need to remember that You're in charge. I have no idea what will happen! Please help me focus on today instead of making all kinds of plans. I want to trust You with my future and do the things You want me to do. I want to do Your will! Amen.

HELP!

In my trouble I called to the Lord; I called to my God for help. In his temple he heard my voice; he listened to my cry for help.
PSALM 18:6 GNT

My Lord and my God, I need Your help! You know what's happening to me. I want to change what has happened, and truly, I'm afraid of what *will* happen. I don't want to live in fear though. And I don't want to live a life of regret. I do need Your help. Thank You for knowing what I need before a word is even out of my mouth— and even when I have no words to describe what I'm thinking and feeling, You know. Thank You for hearing my cry for help. I'm so thankful for You and the way I can trust You completely. In Jesus' name I pray, amen.

FRIEND OF THE WORLD?
OR A FRIEND OF GOD?

*Unfaithful people! Don't you know that to
be the world's friend means to be God's
enemy? If you want to be the world's
friend, you make yourself God's enemy.*
JAMES 4:4 GNT

Father, I apologize for trying to be a friend of
the world. I'm sorry when I forget You and Your
plans and purposes. I focus on things that don't
matter. Instead of trying to be a people pleaser,
I want to please You. I don't want my thoughts
to be filled with things of this world. I don't
want to spend all my time thinking about what
I have or don't have. I don't want to spend my
life figuring out how to be liked by this world.
And I don't want to be Your enemy. I want to
be Your friend. Amen.

WHAT CAN COMPARE?

LORD my God, you have done many miracles.
Your plans for us are many. If I tried to tell
them all, there would be too many to count.
PSALM 40:5 NCV

Father, I'm amazed by You. You created absolutely everything. Everything that has breath lives because of You. You know all. You have a perfect plan for everything—even if I don't understand what that plan is. But I don't have to understand details to worship You and praise You for all You do. Nothing in this world—and no one in this world—compares to You. Your power is mind-boggling. The mercy You've shown me is undeserved and so kind. Thank You! I pray that I'll naturally tell people about You and the good things You've done for me. In Jesus' name I pray, amen.

UNDER PRESSURE

"Stay awake and pray for strength against temptation. The spirit wants to do what is right, but the body is weak."
MATTHEW 26:41 NCV

Father, I had a hard time today. Someone was pressuring me to do something I knew I shouldn't do. The thing is, the temptation seemed pretty appealing. As much as I knew I shouldn't give in, part of me wanted to. What should I do if this happens again, Lord? I know You'll never leave me, no matter what. But because You love me and because I love You, I want to make You happy. And I know obedience to You will make You happy. Please help me not to give in to temptation. Even in my weakness, I want to obey You. Please help me stay strong. Amen.

WHAT I DON'T HAVE

*The LORD gives strength to his people
and blesses them with peace.*
PSALM 29:11 GNT

Father God, tonight I come to You with so much on my mind. And even though it feels like my thoughts are weighing me down, I'm really thankful that You can change my worries to peace. You have a way of filling me with peace like nothing and no one else—and for that, I'm so grateful. You give me strength. When I'm weak, You make me strong. It's incredible that You turn my area of weakness into something great. When I'm tempted to get discouraged, I want to keep my eyes on You. You alone can help me do what I can't manage on my own. I'm so thankful for You and Your peace and strength! In Jesus' name I pray, amen.

FREEDOM!

Live as free people, but do not use your freedom as an excuse to do evil. Live as servants of God.
1 PETER 2:16 NCV

Father, thank You for freedom that comes through Jesus. I can't save myself, no matter what I do. Thank You for saving me! As I enjoy my freedom in Christ, I pray that I won't use it as an excuse to sin and ask for forgiveness afterward. Instead, I want to live as Your servant. With thankfulness for the freedom that comes through You, I pray that I'll make choices that point to You. I don't want to waste my freedom, take it for granted, or misuse it. Please help me treat it as the amazing gift that it is. Thank You for Your true freedom! In Jesus' name I pray, amen.

ONE STEP AT A TIME

Be careful what you do, and always do what is right. Don't turn off the road of goodness; keep away from evil paths.
PROVERBS 4:26–27 NCV

Father, thank You for today. I give tomorrow to You. Please use me as You'd like. I pray that as I make little and big decisions, I'll ponder the way I go. I don't want to just wander around and react to whatever happens to come my way. Please help me stay on the right path—the one You've planned for me. Please steer me away from evil. Please protect me from making foolish choices. I want to live in a way that points others to You, but I need You to please show me what that way is. Please make my footsteps—and all of my choices—firm. In Jesus' name I pray, amen.

LOVE IS THE ANSWER

"You have heard that it was said, 'Love your friends, hate your enemies.' But now I tell you: love your enemies and pray for those who persecute you, so that you may become the children of your Father in heaven."
MATTHEW 5:43–45 GNT

Lord Jesus, Your instruction to love my enemies and pray for those who are mean to me is so hard. It just doesn't feel natural to love when people are hurtful and rude. But I choose to trust You, and I want to obey You. Please help me love people who choose to be my enemies no matter how difficult it may seem. When I'm tempted to act out of hurt and fear, please help me to choose love. Please help me to live like I am a child of my Father in heaven. In Your holy name I pray, amen.

INTENDED FOR GOOD

Then Joseph said to them, "Don't be afraid.
Can I do what only God can do? You meant
to hurt me, but God turned your evil
into good to save the lives of many
people, which is being done."
Genesis 50:19–20 NCV

Father, I love the way You fix what seems so
hopeless in this world. You make things right
that seem so wrong. Just like the way You used
Joseph's awful situation in Egypt to save so
many people, You're also working things out
for good in my life. When people may plan to
harm me, You'll use those moments for good.
You'll work out Your will in my life and in the
world no matter what. For that I'm grateful. And
because of that, I can fall asleep in peace. In
Jesus' name I pray, amen.

SO MUCH LIFE

"The thief [the devil] comes only in order to steal, kill, and destroy. I have come in order that you might have life—life in all its fullness."
JOHN 10:10 GNT

Father, You are the Creator of life. And I know Jesus came so that I might live an overflowing life filled with plenty. But a lot of days, my life doesn't feel so full. It's really easy to get discouraged. I pray that You would open my eyes to see the gift of life. Please help me see how important I am in the lives of other people. And please, even (and especially) when I'm feeling down, show me how I can use my life for You. I pray that You would protect me from Satan and His evil schemes. Please help me live for You! Amen.

TOMORROW IS A NEW DAY

*Sing praise to the L*ord*, all his faithful people!*
Remember what the Holy One has done,
and give him thanks! His anger lasts
only a moment, his goodness for a
lifetime. Tears may flow in the night,
but joy comes in the morning.
P*salm* 30:4–5 gnt

Lord God, I praise You! There is nothing and no one else like You in all of creation. Thank You for Your love and Your favor. Both are undeserved. I couldn't earn any of it on my own. But You've chosen me, and for that I'm grateful! Even when I fall asleep sad or exhausted after a long day, I'm glad I can wake up tomorrow with a fresh start. I may feel heartbroken tonight, but tomorrow morning You can fill me with joy. I pray that I'll find my joy in You. Amen.

THE POWER OF CHOICE

God will reward or punish every person
for what that person has done. Some people,
by always continuing to do good, live for
God's glory, for honor, and for life that
has no end. God will give them life forever.
But other people are selfish. They refuse
to follow truth and, instead, follow evil.
God will give them his punishment and anger.
ROMANS 2:6-8 NCV

Father, every day I'm faced with decisions. It's easy to make choices and forget they mean something. Please help me remember that You'll repay me according to what I do and believe in this life. I want to honor You. I want to bring You glory in all that I do. I want to live by the power of Your Holy Spirit. Please help me live like every moment matters—because it does! In Jesus' name I pray, amen.

THE AUTHOR OF MY STORY

You saw my body as it was formed.
All the days planned for me were written
in your book before I was one day old.
PSALM 139:16 NCV

Father God, You are amazing. You have created all things, including me. And You know all things, including every single moment of my life. You've written the story of my life, one day at a time. And even though certain moments don't make sense to me, they all tie together into a beautiful life. You knew me before my mother knew me. No detail of my life has escaped Your notice. As much as I'd like to know what's in store for me or why certain things have happened—or not happened—I choose to trust in You as the master storyteller. In Jesus' name I pray, amen.

LIVING IN PEACE

Try to live in peace with all people,
and try to live free from sin.
HEBREWS 12:14 NCV

Lord Jesus, You know how difficult it is to live in peace with everyone! Some people on this earth are difficult to get along with. And some people love to stir up trouble. It doesn't matter if it involves lying or fighting—they just want to tear down other people. I don't want to be like that, Lord! As much as it's in my control, I want to be a peacemaker. Please help me live in peace with everyone. I pray that even when it's difficult, I'll try my hardest to bring peace to situations instead of stirring up trouble. In Your name I pray, amen.

THE TREASURE OF WISDOM

*To get wisdom is much better than getting
gold. To get understanding should
be chosen instead of silver.*
PROVERBS 16:16 NLV

Father, You know it's easy for people to focus on money and belongings. According to Your Word, it's always been that way, but it seems like today, more than ever, people obsess over their possessions. I don't want to fall into that trap. When friends seem to get the newest and best of everything, I pray that I wouldn't even want to keep up with them. Please help me remember that certain things are better than riches—like wisdom and understanding! I pray that instead of chasing after money, I'll make wisdom my goal. Please help me to be happy and content with all that You've given me. In Jesus' name I pray, amen.

TRUE LOVE

Most of all, have a true love for each
other. Love covers many sins.
1 PETER 4:8 NLV

Lord Jesus, thank You for living a life of love
here on earth. You loved people so much—and
You were the perfect model of how to be known
by love. Sometimes I don't always feel very
loving. But I pray that I'd love people anyway.
Please help me love those who seem unlovable—
and even people who don't seem to deserve it.
I don't always act lovable, and I don't deserve
Your love. But You love me anyway. And that's
changed my life and my future. Thank You for
covering my sins with Your love. I pray that my
life will reflect Your love and make it obvious
that I'm Yours! In Your name I pray, amen.

MY HIDING PLACE

You are my hiding place.
You keep me safe from trouble.
PSALM 32:7 NLV

Father God, I'm so glad I can hide myself in You! You *are* my hiding place. When bad things are happening all around me, I can find shelter in You. You protect me from trouble. And even if and when I'm hurt, You're still a strong and sure place for me. I'm glad I can run to You. I'm glad You protect me like nothing or no one else. I trust that You'll teach me the way I should go and keep me safe from trouble. Thank You that You are for me and not against me! In Your name I trust and pray, amen.

THINGS OF THE WORLD

Brothers and sisters, this is what I mean:
We do not have much time left.... Those who
buy things should live as if they own nothing.
Those who use the things of the world
should live as if they were not using
them, because this world in its
present form will soon be gone.

1 CORINTHIANS 7:29–31 NCV

Father, it's very easy for me to get distracted by the world and let the things of the world consume my time, energy, and thoughts. I don't want that to happen though. And I don't want to base my happiness on what the world views as happiness. Please help me keep my focus on You. It's in Jesus' name I pray, amen.

PEACEFUL SLEEP

*I go to bed and sleep in peace, because,
LORD, only You keep me safe.*
PSALM 4:8 NCV

Heavenly Father, You are the God of peace.
You've given me peace. And tonight I can and
will lie down and sleep in peace. I don't have
to stay awake in fear, because You're my great
protector, and You have a wonderful plan. I
don't have to worry about what might happen
tonight or tomorrow, because I know You'll
prepare my way. I don't have to toss and turn
all night long, because You keep me safe. Your
protection, safety, and peace are such great
gifts. Thank You! Thank You for the gift of
sweet, peaceful sleep that fills me with energy
and refreshes my spirit. You are so good to me!
In the name of Jesus, the Prince of Peace, I
pray, amen.

EVERYTHING YOU NEED

My God will use his wonderful riches in Christ Jesus to give you everything you need.
PHILIPPIANS 4:19 NCV

Father God, right now I admit I'm worried. I wonder what is coming next and how You'll provide for me. What will happen in school? What kind of job should I have when I grow up? What will happen with my family? Who are my true friends? Will I ever become a wife or mom? For all of my questions, I praise You for being my Provider. You're the God who supplies all my needs. More than anything, I want to trust that You will provide all my needs according to Your wonderful riches in Christ Jesus. Thank You for blessing me so richly—by providing my needs and even some of my wants. I'm so glad I can trust in You! Amen.

LISTEN

The Sovereign LORD has taught me what
to say, so that I can strengthen the weary.
Every morning he makes me eager to
hear what he is going to teach me.
ISAIAH 50:4 GNT

Lord God, I want You to teach me. And I want to follow Your lead. But sometimes I just don't know what You'd like from me! Tomorrow morning could You please wake me up so I can hear You? Please help my ear focus on You and Your truth. I can hardly wait to find out what You want to teach me. I want to learn to listen to You throughout my day. When I'm feeling tired with all the things I need to do, please refresh me. Thank You for always being there for me and always being willing to teach me. In Jesus' name I pray, amen.

HUNGRY? THIRSTY?

Jesus said to them, "I am the Bread of Life.
He who comes to Me will never be hungry.
He who puts his trust in Me will
never be thirsty."
JOHN 6:35 NLV

Lord Jesus, I'm so glad You are the bread of life. Even though You spoke in figures of speech, I'm glad that You alone satisfy a hunger nothing and no one else can. You meet all my needs, and for that I'm so thankful. I pray that I'll stop trying to find comfort in the things of this world, but that I'll live in the freedom that You've given me everything I need. I don't have to worry about this life because life is found in You and You alone. I'm thankful for You and the way You satisfy my soul so completely! In Your name I pray, amen.

WAITING FOR YOU

I waited patiently for the LORD.
He turned to me and heard my cry.
PSALM 40:1 NCV

Father, thank You for hearing my prayers. Thank You for being worthy of being prayed to. I love that I can trust You. And I love the way You have planned what's best for me. I want to be honest though. I've been praying about something for a long time. You know what it is: _____. I keep praying because it's important to me. Please help me to be patient as I wait for You and Your answer. I know Your answer might be yes or no or wait. Oh, the waiting is hard! But no matter what Your answer is and especially in the waiting, I choose to put all of my trust in You. I love You!

PEACE WITH YOU

Now that we have been made right with God by putting our trust in Him, we have peace with Him. It is because of what our Lord Jesus Christ did for us.

ROMANS 5:1 NLV

Father, I'd love to experience peace here in my little corner of the world. And I'd love to experience peace tonight. You want me to experience peace too! But it's impossible for me to have peace right here right now unless I have peace in heaven with You. Jesus came to give peace—not as the world gives, but only as You can give. Thank You that as I ask Jesus to save me and lead my life, I'm made right and at peace with You through Him. Amen.

NEVER FORGET

*"Can a woman forget her nursing child?
Can she have no pity on the son to whom
she gave birth? Even these may forget,
but I will not forget you. See, I have
marked your names on My hands.
Your walls are always before Me."*
ISAIAH 49:15–16 NLV

Lord Jesus, no matter what happens in my life,
I always want to remember certain people. But
as much as I know I *want* to remember people
who are special to me, sometimes a human
brain doesn't work as well as it should and
people are forgotten. Thank You for never, ever
forgetting me. No matter what, You've promised
to remember me. And when You look at Your
nail-scarred hands, You're reminded of me.
Knowing that I matter that much to You amazes
me. Thanks for loving me and caring about me
so very much. Amen.

ALL I NEED TO DO IS ASK

If you do not have wisdom, ask God for it.
He is always ready to give it to you and
will never say you are wrong for asking.
JAMES 1:5 NLV

Father, sometimes I'm so confused. I just don't know what to do. I don't know what Your will is for me and my life. Please give me clear thoughts and help me wisely decide what I should do. I want to honor You with my choices. Thank You for giving generously in everything but especially when it comes to wisdom. I pray that You'll guide me and that I'll listen when You nudge me. As I look to You, please help wise choices to be obvious. And I pray that my soul will rest as I trust You to lead me. In Jesus' name I pray, amen.

WHERE DOES MY HELP COME FROM?

I look up to the hills, but where does my help come from? My help comes from the LORD, who made heaven and earth. He will not let you be defeated. He who guards you never sleeps.
PSALM 121:1-3 NCV

Lord, I need Your help! Right now I want to quit. When life seems hard, it feels easier to give up. But You never quit. And You never stop watching out for me. Thank You for Your nonstop, never-ending help! Thank You for protecting me. You never, ever sleep, so You always know what's going on in my life and everywhere in the whole universe. I'm amazed by how You've created absolutely everything and take care of it all, yet You still love and care for me. You are so worthy of all my honor and praise. Amen.

LIVING IN AN UNBELIEVING WORLD

Happy are you if you are insulted because you are Christ's followers; this means that the glorious Spirit, the Spirit of God, is resting on you.

1 PETER 4:14 GNT

Lord, You know what kind of pressures I face every day. You know how people in this world hate You and say horrible things about You. Comments that I hear about You make me feel sick to my stomach. These truly ugly words only show what's inside of a person's heart, and they so desperately need You to save them. Even when people say bad things about me because of You, I pray that I'll remember that it's actually a blessing. Every insult that comes from being Your follower only reminds me that I'm not of this world. There's more to this life. In Jesus' name I pray, amen.

166

LIFE IS GOOD

*I know that Your goodness and love will
be with me all my life; and your house
will be my home as long as I live.*
PSALM 23:6 GNT

Lord, every day is a gift. On bad days it's hard to
see Your gifts. Please open my eyes to all of the
beauty around me and all of the amazing things
You're working out, whether I'm having a good
or bad day. I know that whatever may happen,
Your goodness and love follow me. Wherever I go,
whatever I do, You surprise me with Your good
gifts. Thank You! Thank You for adding joy to my
life. And thank You that one day You'll welcome
me into Your home to live with You forever. That
will be so much more incredible than I can even
imagine! In Jesus' name I pray, amen.

LIVING LIKE I'M YOUNG

Turn away from the sinful things young people want to do. Go after what is right. Have a desire for faith and love and peace. Do this with those who pray to God from a clean heart.
2 TIMOTHY 2:22 NLV

Father, I know You value my life, and I know You have wonderful plans for me. But Your Word is clear that young people don't always make the wisest choices. If I'm supposed to turn away from the sinful things young people want to do, that means my heart will be pulled in a direction that doesn't honor You. Please give me wisdom to know the difference between right and wrong. Even if it seems difficult or unpopular, please help me go after what is right. Please help me live a life of faith and love and peace. In Jesus' name I pray, amen.

I'M YOUR GIRL

Listen to me, distant nations, you people who live far away! Before I was born, the LORD chose me and appointed me to be his servant.
ISAIAH 49:1 GNT

Lord God, You know I'm Your girl. You knew me before I was created. You know I'm wonderfully made. You called me from my mother's belly. You chose me, and You've delighted in me. This is so amazing to think about! Sometimes I wonder, *Why me?* I'll never know the answer, but You do. Thank You! Thank You for calling me. Thank You for naming me. Thank You for choosing me as Your own. I'm forever grateful. In Jesus' name I pray, amen.

FAITH AND BELIEF

*God makes people right with himself through
their faith in Jesus Christ. This is true for
all who believe in Christ, because all
people are the same.*
ROMANS 3:22 NCV

Father, thank You for Jesus! Thank You that
by believing and having faith in Him, I can be
made right with You. When I'm given a gift, it's
not truly mine until I accept it and make it my
own. I have to take it from the giver and open it.
That's the same with my faith. Jesus isn't truly
mine until I accept Him and make Him my own.
If faith is like a gift, believing in Jesus is a very
real thing to do. I choose to believe with my
mind and my heart. Today I choose to believe
in Jesus and trust that You will make me right
through my faith in Him. Amen.

MAKING LIFE BETTER

Good people will have rich blessings, but the wicked will be overwhelmed by violence.
PROVERBS 10:6 NCV

Father, it's hard to remember that little things I say or do matter to other people. In fact, how I treat people now will change the way they'll always remember me. I want people to smile when they think of me. I don't want others to think bad things whenever they think of me. Even for people who aren't my family or friends, please help me make their lives better just by being myself. I pray that tomorrow You'll use me to make someone's day better. Please help me to be kind. I want my life to reflect Your love. I love You! In Jesus' name I pray, amen.

LISTEN AND DO

*Obey the Word of God. If you hear only and
do not act, you are only fooling yourself.*
JAMES 1:22 NLV

Lord God, Your Word is true. It's living and active. It can judge my thoughts and my heart's intentions. It can guide me—if I'll let it. Thank You for the gift of Your Word. I pray that I won't forget about it. I pray that I won't just listen to it and then do my own thing. I want to do what Your Word asks. As it guides me, please give me strength and courage to follow what it says. I want what You say—even if and when it seems difficult. Please help me find what Your Word says, base my life on it, and put it into action. It's a great gift, and I'm thankful for it. Amen.

PRAISE THE LORD!

I will always thank the LORD;
I will never stop praising him.
PSALM 34:1 GNT

Father God, I praise You! You created all things. You faithfully protect and provide for Your children. You have a plan for all of time and eternity. Nothing escapes Your notice and nothing surprises You. Even when I feel like I don't have much faith, You are faithful. Even when I feel like I don't have much love, You are loving. Even when sin separated humans from Your perfection, You made a way of forgiveness and mercy through Jesus. Thank You! I needed to be saved! Your awesomeness is so much more than I can ever comprehend! With much praise for You I pray. Amen.

WHAT IS LOVE?

Love is patient and kind. Love is not jealous, it does not brag, and it is not proud. Love is not rude, is not selfish, and does not get upset with others. Love does not count up wrongs that have been done. Love takes no pleasure in evil but rejoices over the truth. Love patiently accepts all things. It always trusts, always hopes, and always endures. Love never ends.
1 Corinthians 13:4–8 NCV

Father, Your love is patient and kind. It continues forever. It changes the world, and it has changed my heart and my life. When I think of Your love, my own love doesn't measure up. In fact, I feel very unloving compared to You. I want to be known as a loving girl. Please fill me with Your Spirit and let Your love spill out to all who are around me. Amen.

VANISHED!

As far as the east is from the west,
so far does he remove our sins from us.
PSALM 103:12 GNT

Lord, You know my sins. Tonight, I come to You and confess what I've done. Please forgive me. Knowing that You completely remove my sins amazes me. They've vanished! You've removed them as far as the east is from the west, infinitely far! Thank You for Your forgiveness. Please help me turn from my sin and walk the other way. Through Your Holy Spirit, please help me live in obedience to You. I want to please You in everything I say and do. In Jesus' name I pray, amen.

THINK ABOUT THIS. . .

Think about the things that are good and worthy of praise. Think about the things that are true and honorable and right and pure and beautiful and respected.

PHILIPPIANS 4:8 NCV

Lord, sometimes it's so hard to think about good things! Surrounded by the mess of this world, it's hard to focus on what's true. Honorable things seem hard to come by. The line between right and wrong seems blurry. Purity? It's like it's vanishing. And things that are beautiful, respected, and praiseworthy can be hard to find. But I'm still asked to think about those things. So, I pray that I might find them in the everyday moments of life. Please help me delight in what's good, true, honorable, right, pure, beautiful, respected, and praiseworthy. I'd love to be surprised by them tomorrow and celebrate them as gifts from You. Amen.

GREAT THINGS

The LORD has done great things for us,
and we are very glad.
PSALM 126:3 NCV

Lord, You have done great things for me! You've chosen me. You've called me Your own. You've opened my eyes and heart to Your truth. You've rescued me through Christ. All of those great things make me joyful. They give me hope and a future. They comfort me when life feels stressful. Thank You that I can trust You completely with my entire future. Joy is a wonderful gift that comes from You. Thank You for the way it fills my soul and overflows to every part of my life. I pray that it would be contagious to the people around me as You help me to tell others about the great things You've done. In Jesus' name I pray, amen.

CONTENTMENT!

*A God-like life gives us much when we are
happy for what we have. We came into this
world with nothing. For sure, when we die,
we will take nothing with us. If we have
food and clothing, let us be happy.*
1 TIMOTHY 6:6–8 NLV

Father, I pray that I'll be content with all You've
given me. It's easy to get caught up in thinking
about what I wish I had. Why do I always seem
to want more? Please help me remember that
I didn't bring a single thing with me into this
world when I was born. And when I die, I won't
take anything with me. Please help me focus
on being more like You instead of focusing
on material things. When I'm more like You,
I become more content. And when I become
more like You, I can take that with me. Amen.

WATCHFUL PROTECTION

The LORD will guard you; he is by your side to protect you. The sun will not hurt you during the day, nor the moon during the night.
PSALM 121:5-6 GNT

Lord God, You are so good to me! With You, I don't have to fear. Thank You for watching over me all day and all night long. I don't have to worry about harm—not in the light of day and not in the dark of night. I don't have to worry about getting scorched by things of this world—You're my shade! Please continue to watch over me, especially when I'm scared by what people try to do to me. Please protect me from the evil plans and harm from people. I know You watch over me—please keep me safe! In the strong name of Jesus I pray, amen.

LIGHT INSTEAD OF DARKNESS

*Jesus spoke to all the people, saying,
"I am the Light of the world. Anyone who
follows Me will not walk in darkness.
He will have the Light of Life."*
JOHN 8:12 NLV

Lord Jesus, You are the Light of the World! I'm thankful that because of You I don't have to walk in darkness. Thank You for giving me the light of life, because light drives away darkness. When darkness and fear threaten to steal my focus, I pray that I'll keep my mind on You. Thanks also for the amazing ways You light my path. If I stick with You and stop trying to go my own way, You'll lead me moment by moment. I may not know what's coming up, but You do. And as long as I stick with You, You'll make everything clear. In Your name I pray, amen.

WHAT CAN PEOPLE DO?

I trust in God. I will not be afraid.
What can people do to me?
PSALM 56:11 NCV

Father, I'm glad I can come to You with anything. Sometimes I get scared about what's happening in the world. I know You didn't create humans to live this way—everything changed once sin entered the picture in the Garden of Eden. But it's good to know that even if and when people intend to harm others, Your purposes and plans will stand! Your name is a strong tower for those who trust You. I do trust You! And when I run to Your name, I am safe. Please help me to bravely shine Your light in this dark world, to change my corner of the world with Your love. Please help me boldly stand for You. Amen.

HONOR

Respect your father and mother. This is the first Law given that had a promise. The promise is this: If you respect your father and mother, you will live a long time and your life will be full of many good things.
EPHESIANS 6:2–3 NLV

Father, sometimes I get so angry with my parents. I don't always understand why You chose this family for me! Even though I get frustrated, please help me see the ways they're a blessing to me. I pray they might understand me and where I'm coming from—and that I might, in some way, understand them and their perspective too. I know You want me to honor them. And I know I should. So even when I don't feel like doing that, please help me. Please help me appreciate what they're doing and learn from them too. Amen.

YOU ARE GREAT!

May all who come to you be glad and joyful.
May all who are thankful for your salvation
always say, "How great is the LORD!"
PSALM 40:16 GNT

Lord, You are great! And I rejoice in You. It's an amazing thing to know You—and be known by You. You make me glad—from the tips of my toes to the top of my head! Sometimes my heart feels like it could burst with Your joy. Thank You for Your saving help! Thank You that I'm never alone. Please help me remember that all I need to do is seek You and I'll find You. I pray that tomorrow I'll think about Your greatness all day long and that it will change the way I live. I love You! In Jesus' name I pray, amen.

DOING WHAT'S RIGHT

*For what credit is there if you endure the
beatings you deserve for having done wrong?
But if you endure suffering even when you
have done right, God will bless you for it.*
1 PETER 2:20 GNT

Father, it's hard to make decisions between
right and wrong every single day. But I want to
do what's right, no matter what. Even if people
make fun of me or threaten to do bad things to
me, even if people make my life miserable, I still
want to do what is right. If I have to suffer for
it, please help me suffer patiently. I need Your
help to do this! It will be hard but so worth it.
Making the right choices—no matter what—is
something You want me to do. And that's what
I want to do. In Jesus' name I pray, amen.

WHAT IS BEAUTY?

Charm can fool you, and beauty can trick
you, but a woman who respects
the LORD should be praised.
PROVERBS 31:30 NCV

Lord, every day I think about beauty in some way. Am I beautiful enough? How can I look better? It's frustrating. I want to be beautiful, but sometimes I feel plain. Help me remember that You don't see beauty the same way humans do. You look at a person's heart, not at appearances. And what is beautiful in the heart is someone who respects You. Father, I pray that You'll help me realize that true beauty is what I'm like on the inside—and help me become totally beautiful in that way. Please help my love for You and faith in You to shine out to others around me. In Jesus' name I pray, amen.

THE HOPE OF GLORY

God decided to let his people know this rich and glorious secret which he has for all people. This secret is Christ himself, who is in you. He is our only hope for glory.
<small>COLOSSIANS 1:27 NCV</small>

Father God, realizing that You chose to make Yourself known to me in the closest way—Christ *in* me—is almost too much to understand. But once Jesus Christ became my Lord and Savior, He began living in me. That's mysterious and mind-blowing and marvelous. He's not distant but right there. Christ living inside of me is the hope of glory. I pray that I'll live a changed life knowing this hope for glory. And I pray that I'll live worthy of all the riches You've so generously given me. In Jesus' precious name I pray, amen.

ARE YOU WITH ME?

The LORD was with Joseph and made him successful in everything he did.
GENESIS 39:23 NCV

Father, Your Word is filled with great stories of what happened to men and women thousands of years ago. Even if it seems like ancient history to me, I can still learn lessons from their lives and the ways You worked through them. It's wonderful that Joseph was a man who trusted You. It's encouraging that You were with Him no matter what. Even when he had every right to despair about his future, You were with him, giving him success. I may not be locked up in a prison, Lord, but I pray that You'll be with me too. Please bless what I say and do. Please give me success in whatever I do. I pray that I'll do everything for You. In Jesus' name I pray, amen.

FOCUS ON THE GOOD

Be full of joy all the time. Never stop praying.
In everything give thanks. This is what God
wants you to do because of Christ Jesus.
1 THESSALONIANS 5:16–18 NLV

Father, I love that Your will for me is to be full of joy! And to pray to You! And to thank You for everything. What a wonderful will for my life. This world can drag me down so easily. But You never intended that for me. You intend to bring life. And You want me to live a life that overflows with joy. When I have bad days, I pray that I'll turn to You in prayer and choose to thank You. Please help me focus on the wonderful things that are happening even right now and experience true freedom that comes through You! In Christ Jesus' name I pray, amen.

ALL I NEED

What else do I have in heaven but you?
Since I have you, what else could I want on
earth? My mind and my body may grow weak,
but God is my strength; he is all I ever need.
PSALM 73:25-26 GNT

Lord, You are all I need. There's nothing else
on this earth I truly want except for You. Every
day, things and people try to rob my attention
and affection from You, but I know nothing
else can compare to You. Not any other relationship. Not any belonging. Not any award
or honor or opportunity. You and You alone
are the true strength of my heart. Everything
and everyone else might fall away, but I'll still
have You. Please help me to keep my focus
on You and not on the stuff of this world. In
Jesus' name I pray, amen.

FORGETTING WHAT'S BEHIND

*The one thing I do, however, is to forget what
is behind me and do my best to reach what
is ahead. So I run straight toward the goal
in order to win the prize, which is God's call
through Christ Jesus to the life above.*
PHILIPPIANS 3:13–14 GNT

Jesus, You've promised me a great prize. As I've trusted You with my life and believe that You are my living Savior, You've promised me an eternity with You! A reward instead of punishment. Life with You instead of separation. A changed heart and soul. I pray that I'll forget about the things of this world. Instead, I want to live in Your freedom. I want to run straight toward Your amazing prize every day, remembering that You're my Lord and that You've called me as Your own. In Your name I pray, amen.

NIGHTMARES

*"It was during a nightmare when people are
in deep sleep. I was trembling with fear;
all my bones were shaking."*
JOB 4:13-14 NCV

Father, sometimes I'm afraid to fall asleep because of nightmares. I hate being so scared at night. I don't know why I've been having so many bad dreams lately, but could You please bless me with good dreams tonight? I don't want to be afraid. And I don't want to fear falling asleep. Please help me trust You, and please protect me tonight—both my body and my mind. Even in my sleep, please help me remember that You love and care for me. Amen.

RIGHT VS. WRONG

*If God wants you to suffer, it is better
to suffer for doing what is right
than for doing what is wrong.*
1 Peter 3:17 nlv

Father, even though I can feel so pressured by people around me, I want to please You more than anyone else. Would You please give me strength to follow Your commands and live like Your daughter? Could You please help me make the right decisions instead of choosing wrong ones? Even if people make fun of me, purposely overlook me because of my belief in You, or even try to hurt me, I pray that You'll protect me and remind me that You're the One I want to please. You are the ultimate Judge. And You are the one true God. I love You and want to spend my life honoring You, no matter what. In Jesus' name I pray, amen.

WHITE AS SNOW

"Come now, let us think about this together,"
says the Lord. "Even though your sins are
bright red, they will be as white as snow.
Even though they are dark red,
they will be like wool."
ISAIAH 1:18 NLV

Lord Jesus, I'm glad the Bible is filled with such great descriptions. My sins *are* bright red. I'm guilty, and it's like my sin has stained me. But You've taken that away. Your forgiveness washes me and turns me into a brand-new creation. Through Your sacrifice for me, I'm clean. In Your eyes, my stain is gone, and now I'm white as snow. You've saved me. You've forgiven my sins. And my guilt and shame are gone! I can never thank You enough for Your amazing gift. You are so good to me! In Your name I pray, amen.

BECOMING A PEACEMAKER

*"Happy are those who work for peace;
God will call them his children!"*
MATTHEW 5:9 GNT

Lord Jesus, You brought peace to this world through Your life and Your death. And You've brought peace to me! Please help me live peacefully with other people around me. I pray that instead of stirring up trouble, I will be a calming person. Even when people would rather lash out in anger or hate, I pray that I will react peacefully. If I try to bring peace to a situation, please help me know that's all You ask of me. My peace may not be received well, but I can still try. Like You, I can offer peace. Not everyone accepts Your peace, yet You still offer it. I'll gladly take Your peace with a thankful heart. I love You, Jesus! In Your name I pray, amen.

LOAD CARRIER

Honor and thanks be to the Lord,
Who carries our heavy loads day by
day. He is the God Who saves us.
PSALM 68:19 NLV

Father, You are my God, and Jesus is my Savior. Thank You that I'm not alone in this life—You share it with me. And every day You carry my burdens. Even when I'm feeling weighed down, You pick up my heavy load and take it for me. You don't leave me to struggle on my own. I'm relieved to know You're with me and You'll shoulder what's weighing me down. Jesus promised that if I would come to Him, I'd find rest. I do come to Him! I pray that I'll find freedom, relief, and rest in Him. Thank You for releasing me from the weight of this world. I love finding freedom and peace in You. In Jesus' name I pray, amen.

BE CHOOSY

Remember this, my dear friends! Everyone must be quick to listen, but slow to speak and slow to become angry. Human anger does not achieve God's righteous purpose.
JAMES 1:19-20 GNT

Lord Jesus, please watch over my mouth! Blurting out what I'm thinking happens so easily. Or even worse, I start talking without even really thinking about what I'm saying. I'm embarrassed by what I've said simply because I haven't thought about the words I've used. Please help me to be a better listener—and to be quick to listen instead of thinking about what I want to say in response. Please help me watch over my mouth and emotions, and please help me to be slow when it comes to getting angry. It's hard, but through You and Your power I know it's possible. In Your name I pray, amen.

WHO'S IN CONTROL?

People, trust God all the time. Tell him all your problems, because God is our protection.
PSALM 62:8 NCV

Father, tonight I need to remember that You're in control and You're my protection. I'm so glad You are, because I feel like everything is out of my control. Please help me rest and trust in the fact that You know so much more about what is going on—and so much more of what I actually need and what is for my good. Deep down I'm scared to let go of my hopes and dreams and place them in Your hands. But I know that I need to—and I want to give them to You. Please fill me with Your peace as I trust You with my problems and my life. In Jesus' name I pray, amen.

MAKING THE MOST OF EVERY OPPORTUNITY

So be very careful how you live. Do not live like those who are not wise, but live wisely. Use every chance you have for doing good, because these are evil times.
EPHESIANS 5:15–16 NCV

Lord Jesus, I want to be careful with the way I live. Because of this, it's important that I wisely make day-to-day decisions. Please help me! All the little choices I make add up. Every day is filled with opportunities to follow You, obey what You command, and show Your love to the world around me. Please help me to be a good example for You with the words I say, in my attitudes, and in the way I treat other people. Please help me bring Your love to those who need it the most. In Your name I pray, amen.

198

COMFORT AND JOY

You will say on that day, "I will give thanks to You, O Lord. Even though You were angry with me, Your anger is turned away and You comfort me. See, God saves me. I will trust and not be afraid. For the Lord God is my strength and song. And He has become the One Who saves me." As water from a well brings joy to the thirsty, so people have joy when He saves them.

ISAIAH 12:1-3 NLV

Lord, You saved me! And You comfort me. Thank You! I'm so happy I don't have to fear anymore since I've trusted You. I'm relieved Your anger is turned away from me. Instead of being angry, You bring comfort. You give me strength. And You fill me with joy! I pray that Your joy will shine in my life. In Jesus' name I pray, amen.

NEVER LEFT ALONE

Keep your lives free from the love of money.
Be happy with what you have. God has said,
"I will never leave you or let you be alone."
HEBREWS 13:5 NLV

Lord, thank You for keeping Your promises. I know that when You promise You will never leave me, it's true. It's so comforting to know I'm never alone. Sometimes, though, it's hard to imagine You never, ever leaving me—not even for a split second. But a promise is a promise, and You always keep Your promises. Please help me to be happy with what You give me. Even when I think I know what I want—or when I want something different than You give—please help me not to be ungrateful. Thank You for what I have. In Jesus' name I pray, amen.

I'M A GIFT!

Children are a gift from the LORD;
they are a real blessing.
PSALM 127:3 GNT

Father, I'm amazed that I am a gift from You! I'm a real blessing! Some days I don't feel like much of a gift. And when my parents and I don't get along, I don't feel like I bless their lives. But it doesn't matter how I feel. What matters is that You see me as special. You've created me just the way I am for a special reason. I may not know or understand Your reason, but You do! And You created me to bless others. That's a little surprising to me and completely awesome. Thank You! In Jesus' name I pray, amen.

WALK IN LOVE

Live a life of love just as Christ loved us and gave himself for us as a sweet-smelling offering and sacrifice to God.
EPHESIANS 5:2 NCV

Father, Your Word tells me that You are love. When Jesus was on earth, He commanded His disciples to love each other as He had loved them. I know I need to love others. Sometimes I want to love other people, but other times I don't. Please help me to do it! Tomorrow, please open my eyes and show me how I can live a life of love. Give me eyes to see people around me who need Your love, and then give me the strength and courage to love them well. In Jesus' name I pray, amen.

SHOW ME THE WAY

Remind me each morning of your constant love, for I put my trust in you. My prayers go up to you; show me the way I should go.
PSALM 143:8 GNT

Lord, when I get distracted by my life, it's easy to forget about Your constant love. But You really do love me all the time. Even when I forget about You. Not only do You love me, but You also listen to me and my prayers. When I wake up tomorrow morning, please remind me of Your love. And as I go about my day, please show me the way I should go. I'd love to know what You think I should do and say! Please help me to listen well and to obey what You ask. I love You, Lord! Amen.

HARD TO BE HUMBLE

*Humble yourselves before the Lord,
and He will lift you up.*
JAMES 4:10 GNT

Father, tonight I come to You humbled. It's not easy to lower myself—so often it's easier to think pretty highly of myself and to puff myself up. But I want to take my eyes off of myself. I want to stop thinking great things about me and realize exactly what I am: a girl who desperately needs her Lord. Help me remember who I am—and who You are. You are in control of everything, and I'm not. You're loving and just and filled with mercy. If I'm honest with myself, I struggle every day. I wish I were more loving. I would like to be more just and merciful to others. Please help me! In Jesus' name I pray, amen.

CHOOSING MY FRIENDS

Happy are those who don't listen to the wicked, who don't go where sinners go, who don't do what evil people do. They love the LORD's teachings, and they think about those teachings day and night.
PSALM 1:1–2 NCV

Lord, I pray that You'll give me wisdom when it comes to choosing my friends! I really don't want to spend time with the wicked because I don't want their habits to rub off on me. I want to make wise choices when it comes to my friends! Please surround me with people who love You. I pray that my friends and I could help each other grow closer to You. Please help us to know Your Word better and better and encourage each other to live out Your truth in what we say and do. I'm excited to see the friends You'll bring into my life! Amen.

WE ARE FAMILY

He gave the right and the power to become children of God to those who received Him. He gave this to those who put their trust in His name. These children of God were not born of blood and of flesh and of man's desires, but they were born of God.
JOHN 1:12–13 NLV

Father, I'm so thankful You've given people the right to become Your children. Even though not everyone accepts that right, You've still invited everyone. I'll gladly take Your invitation! I receive Christ and trust in His name. As I do that, I'm thankful that I'm born of You—as Your daughter. It hasn't depended on what I have or haven't done. It's Your will and Yours alone. And it's Your amazing gift to me. Thank You! I'm so glad I'm part of Your family! In Jesus' name I pray, amen.

BE STRONG AND BRAVE

*"Be strong and brave. Don't be afraid of them and don't be frightened, because the L*ORD *your God will go with you. He will not leave you or forget you."*
DEUTERONOMY 31:6 NCV

Lord God, I'm so glad I can be strong and brave in You! I don't have to be afraid or frightened of anything or anyone. Every single day You go with me everywhere! And You never leave me or forget me. If I start feeling scared, please remind me that You're with me. You can and will give me strength. Through You and Your power, I can be brave. Thank You! In Jesus' name I pray, amen.

EVERY SPIRITUAL BLESSING

Praise be to the God and Father of our Lord Jesus Christ. In Christ, God has given us every spiritual blessing in the heavenly world.
EPHESIANS 1:3 NCV

God and Father of my Lord Jesus Christ, I praise You! You are so holy. You are so powerful. You have such an amazing plan. And You have chosen to bless me with much more than I can ever imagine or deserve. To realize that my blessings are in the heavenly realms is something I can't even wrap my brain around. And the fact that You've blessed me with every spiritual blessing in Christ?! I pray that I'll celebrate and rest in these truths when I'm tempted to feel bogged down by the stuff of everyday life. Thank You for Your incredible gifts! In my Lord Jesus Christ's name I pray, amen.